CW00536294

When we Lived at Primrose Hill

When we Lived at Primrose Hill

Recollections of a Childhood in the Chilterns

Diana Farmbrough

Matador
Unit E2 Airfield Business Park,
Harrison Road, Market Harborough,
Leicestershire. LE16 7UL
Tel: 0116 2792299
Email: books@troubador.co.uk
Web: www.troubador.co.uk/matador
Twitter: @matadorbooks

ISBN 978 1803137 001

British Library Cataloguing in Publication Data.
A catalogue record for this book is available from the British Library.

Typeset in 11pt Adobe Garamond Pro by Troubador Publishing Ltd, Leicester, UK

Matador is an imprint of Troubador Publishing Ltd

This book is dedicated to my great niece
Ada
and to the next generation of our extended family
— the future keepers of these stories.

Contents

This book contains recollections from my childhood in the Chilterns. It is an attempt to reach a version of the truth, but it is not the whole picture, and therefore accuracy is not vouchsafed. Where necessary names have been changed.

Readers will detect my love of natural history and the countryside. It thus seemed appropriate to support the work of the Chiltern Society in their efforts to protect the beautiful, precious, and fragile landscape of the Chiltern Hills for future generations. All profits from sales of this book will be donated to this excellent charity.

1

March 2020 – Lockdown Fantasy –
How It All Began – Grayson Perry at My Doorstep

It was a beautiful spring morning, the pandemic had just begun. There was a knock at the door. Who should be there but Grayson Perry, dressed as Claire. He was wearing a stunning yellow frilled dress, big puff sleeves and a blue and white sash, a matching ribbon in his hair, and yellow and blue platform shoes tied with similar matching ribbons. His make-up and hair were out of this world. At his side was a tall cardboard box.

"I didn't expect to see you here," I said. "Why have you come?"

He laughed, flicked back his hair, and said,

"I've brought you one of my pots decorated with images from your childhood."

I found that very hard to believe, but sure enough, when he handed over the box, inside there was a three-foot-high vase and on it were transfer pictures of our family home, Finchers, Primrose Hill, and there were Mum, Dad, my sister Mary and Grampy standing at the gate. There were separate transfers for our cat Nipper in the wheelbarrow, the rabbit hutches behind the garden shed and our swing on the back lawn. Turning the vase, I viewed our back garden with fruit bushes on the left side of the path and rows of vegetables on the right. At the end was the new hen house for our Rhode Island Reds and a row of sunflower plants, the flowers almost ripe, and ready to feed them.

My heart leapt, and I was momentarily transported back to the happy days of my childhood. With tears in my eyes, I said:

"I can't thank you enough, Grayson."

He replied:

"Don't worry, a lot of people have this reaction to my work."

So, I plucked up the courage to ask him if he could tell me what he understood about the value of self-revelation through Art, but at that moment people were passing, and the two-metre coronavirus restrictions came between us, so Grayson said:

"You will have to leave that one with me, but I promise to send you a transcript of my Reith Lectures, when they're broadcast."

Then off he flounced.

2

Coming to Finchers

This set of stories is about the first eleven years of my life. It describes the small, enclosed world I lived in with my parents, my sister Mary, and our Great Grandfather, "Grampy Rackstraw". It covers the time between 1945 and 1955 when we lived at Finchers, Primrose Hill, Widmer End – a two-bedroomed, bay-windowed bungalow built between the wars.

Widmer End was a remote village outside High Wycombe nestled in the southern Chiltern Hills in Buckinghamshire. A bus service ran four times a day and terminated at the foot of the hill. Residents and visitors had to walk the rest of the way to the houses further up the hill. As was common in the rounded Chilterns, there were no houses on the hill itself: it was easier to build on the flatter land at the top.

Although Primrose Hill was isolated, we were far from alone. Less than a mile away lived our father's father, known to us as "Grampy Farmbrough"; he had lived in Hazlemere all his adult life, and had been a widower since 1932. He was a tall, elegant figure, smartly dressed in jacket, collar and tie and a cloth cap. During the summer months he sported a garden rose as a buttonhole. He was an established and well-regarded member of the Hazlemere community; most of his ten children having been pupils at Hazlemere Church of England School, attended the local Sunday School, and sung in Hazlemere Holy Trinity Church Choir, where Grampy still sang. Although his voice was more mature, it was deep and mellow and he could hold a tune.

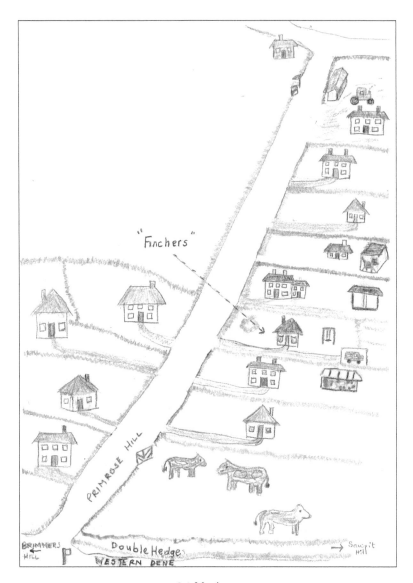

2.1 Mary's map

He had built The Coppice for
his growing family during the
"Roaring Twenties", when he
was working in the furniture
trade in High Wycombe. By the
late 1940s, when all the uncles
had returned from the War, he
now shared the bungalow with
his unmarried son, our uncle
David, home from the Navy,
our Dad's twin sister, Pauline,
her husband Reg (home from
the Royal Air Force) and their
son Geoffrey.

2.2 Grampy Farmbrough

We visited at least once
a week. To walk to his house
entailed going down Primrose Hill, along Western Dene, always
referred to as "the bottom" and halfway up Holmer Green Road towards
Hazlemere. Our legs usually ached by the time we got there, and we
were glad to share a chair at the dining table in Grampy's kitchen:

"Grampy, please can we see Rupert Bear?"

Rupert Bear (who wore a red jumper and yellow checked trousers)
was a cartoon series in the *Daily Express*, and we enjoyed following the
adventures with his chums, an elephant called Edward Trunk and a
Pekingese dog called Algy Pug, while the adults talked.

Grampy Farmbrough was the central contact for news and gossip
about our Farmbrough relations. There were a lot to keep up with!
Apart from our father's brothers and sisters, my sister and I were
surrounded by eleven first cousins, children of our father's siblings,
living in the surrounding villages. A further two lived in London. Our
sister Hilary and one more cousin, Richard, were born ten years later.

Mary and I had no living grandmothers, which didn't unduly
bother us at the time, although I recall asking some cousins whether
we could share one of theirs. Later in life we realised how much we had
missed from the extra security and emotional support a grandmother
would have added to our lives.

2.3 Finchers, Primrose Hill

If you came to visit, and climbed up Primrose Hill, you would find Finchers was the fifth property, among bungalows of a similar age, on the right-hand side. The garden path was on the right and southern side – it led past the two bay windows, the further being our parent's bedroom and the nearer the front room, which also had a window alongside the path. A visitor would bypass the front door (it was hardly ever used) and continue past the south-facing kitchen window, then round the corner to the left where there was a porch over the back door.

The back door opened directly into the kitchen, the warm and sunny heart of our home. Opposite the door was the fireplace, a newly installed cream-enamelled Courtier Stove with a long hot plate and a large oven. There was always a fire in the kitchen and this provided hot running water for the kitchen and bathroom, something not at all common in 1945 when we first moved in.

"Hot and Cold Running Water and all Modern Conveniences" brought forth a sigh of satisfaction from our parents and gritted teeth and grimaces from some of our neighbours and relations, who had no intention of changing their arrangements, but didn't like to be reminded.

Three armchairs were arranged round the fire: Grampy's Windsor chair on the left and our parents' more modern semi-upholstered chairs in front and to the right. On the left of Grampy's chair and under the window was the kitchen table and chairs. This table was a real worktop, covered with oil cloth, not just for meals (when a proper tablecloth was brought out), but for writing letters, making cakes and pastry, ironing, cutting out dress patterns and working with the sewing machine, wrapping parcels and making jam, chutneys, pickles and preserves.

In the corner to the left of the back door was a set of four utility cupboards. The lowest was allocated as our Toy Cupboard, though by the end of the war there were very few toys available. I was given a nineteen-year-old teddy bear who lived in my bed and my sister a sheepskin homemade teddy. We loved our teddies and were glad to snuggle up with them at bedtime. I had a sheepskin rabbit (who had lost his ears); we shared a wooden horse on wheels, a metal wind-up musical box, a humming spinning top and a couple of other clockwork toys; crayons and colouring books were part of our hoard. We had a few ancient books such as *Aesop's Fables*, from which we selected our bedtime stories.

"Please Dad, tell us the story of The Dog in the Manger… The Hare and the Tortoise…"

The next cupboard up was for medicines, cough linctus, syrup of figs, milk of magnesia and other foul-tasting tinctures; the only nice thing that came from that cupboard was Virol (a malt extract), and we were allowed a spoonful each before going out on a cold winter's day.

"Can I lick the spoon?"… "No, it's my turn!"

The cupboard above was for the iron and ironing blanket, useful tools, brown paper, string, and sealing wax. The top cupboard contained dry groceries, currants, flour, junket, and marmite. The wireless was in pride of place on top of this set of cupboards, usually tuned to the Light Programme and generally on for most of the day. In the mornings, after a special introductory tune, came:

"Time for Music While You Work!"

To the right of the back door under an east-facing window was the sink, draining boards on either side and draining rack hanging from the wall of the larder. Everything that needed to be kept cool was in the larder: milk bottles in a pail of water on the quarry tiled floor, butter, lard, and eggs; fridges were not in common use. Arranged along the larder shelves were jars of pickled onions, beetroot, preserved fruit from the garden, different flavoured jams and chutneys, all homemade by our mother, and some growing a crusty mould on top (Mum would rebuff any derogatory comments, saying, "You've got to eat a peck* before you die," as she deftly removed the waxed disc on top of the jar, taking most of the mould with it). The bathroom led off the kitchen, and between the bathroom and the door to the hall was an electric stove, deemed too expensive and unreliable, due to the high cost of electricity and unpredictable power cuts.

The floor of the kitchen was covered in brown linoleum and there was a large woven coconut mat in front of the fire. Visitors meant the kettle would go on the hob, and in no time, a welcoming cup of tea was ready to serve.

---

*   *Peck: a measure of dry volume; a proverb meaning eating a small amount of food briefly exposed to slightly unsanitary conditions won't be harmful in the long run.*

3

Grampy Rackstraw

Edmund Rackstraw was born in 1861 and after my birth in 1944, I was lucky enough to share the last six years of his life. He was my mother's grandfather on her mother's side.

He was an important part of our household: Mum, Dad, Grampy, me and my sister Mary (born 1945). To our parents he was a help with the odd jobs and gardening; to me he was a deep feeling of warmth, comfort and belonging. Grampy was always there; he kept an eye out for us playing in the garden, and indoors, he was always a welcome knee to sit or sleep on.

3.1 Grampy Rackstraw

To us as children he seemed adult-sized, but in reality Grampy wasn't very tall; he had a thatch of sparse white hair and a white moustache. He wore a long black Edwardian jacket and striped trousers. Beneath the jacket was his buttoned-up waistcoat with his pocket watch and chain across the buttons. When his shirt did not have a collar attached, he wore a kerchief around his neck.

He kept a tin of tobacco in one pocket and his pipe and matches* in the other. He always had a pen knife on him, and I remember going with him at mid-day to cut one or two shallots from the string of onions in the woodshed to accompany his meal.

At the age of just fourteen, and in order to escape rural poverty and hunger, he joined the militia as a medical orderly, which took him to South Africa, where he experienced horror, trauma and inhumanity, resulting in his life long and resolute pacifism. He left the militia and by the time he was nineteen was back in Hazlemere. In later life, a strong bond was formed between our mum, Sybil, an orphan, and Grampy. He lost his wife Annie Maria, after forty-five years of marriage, when Sybil was only ten years old.

To my sister and me he was very old (eighty-two when I was born) and we knew he cared deeply for our little family. Grampy tended our vegetable garden and was always busy weeding and hoeing, and he was always there if we became upset. He spoke with a broad Bucks accent, which I could understand, but I knew it was different from how other people spoke.

---

* *Grampy kept his matches in a Vesta, still in our sister Hilary's possession. It is an upright silver case to hold his match box with a rough striking surface at the base. He had been using matches and smoking before the introduction of safety matches.*

4

Our Mum – Sybil Tells a Story about a Plague of Frogs

By 1949, Pete and I had been married for 7 years. We now owned our first real home, Finchers, which felt like a dream come true. When I look back on that spring, I realise how happy and contented I was with the way things had worked out for our little family.

Grampy, who was my nearest surviving relation, had continued to live with us after our marriage. We had two daughters, Diana now nearly six years old, and Mary four and a half. These lovely little girls were the light of our lives. We yearned for and intended to give them so many opportunities denied us when we were growing up. There was reason to be optimistic, the uncertainties of the War were receding, flour and clothes had come off the ration, and we were hopeful other shortages like butter, tinned fruit, soap, petrol and sugar would follow. Pete had a good job and worked hard, and Grampy tended our vegetable and fruit garden; we kept rabbits and chickens and we were coping pretty well.

One Monday morning in March, the weather was bright and windy, a good washing day. As usual, Pete kissed us goodbye before going off to work, and then I prepared breakfast for the girls and Grampy and put jacket potatoes in the Courtier Stove for our midday meal. After breakfast, the girls went out to play, Grampy went to the shed and took out a hoe to work in the garden. The washing was well underway, when Allan Tilly, the tubby son of our neighbours, came round to the back door and said:

"Please Mrs. Farmbrough, can Diana and Mary come with me an' the Bennells to play at the top of the road?"

He was a well-mannered boy and neatly dressed; he often played with the girls and the three Bennell children. The top of the road was no more than a quarter of a mile away and there was next to no traffic. The children had been up there before, and so I said:

"Yes but be careful not to go any further."

So off they went.

I was just pegging out the washing when back came the girls.

"Mum, Mum, can we have a jam jar to collect frogspawn? We've found loads of it in the pond at Hawbushes Farm."

Thinking about the possible drawbacks and playing for time, I said:

"I'm not sure I have any spare jam jars and anyway what if you break one and cut yourselves?"

Not to be put off, they soon found the box in the shed where the empty jam jars were kept and returned with one each. I was slightly envious because watching frogspawn develop was something I had never had the opportunity to do as a child.

By this time Grampy, who had been resting, smoking his pipe in his Windsor chair in the kitchen, came out to see what all the excitement was, and asked:

"What be agoin' on then, me little ducks?"

I told him:

"They want to bring some frogspawn home in jam jars," but Grampy could see the problem of where to keep them and said:

"That be no good, they frogs lives in ponds, there bain't no water for 'em here."

I loved Grampy wholeheartedly, and hated to cross him but how could I refuse the bright-eyed enthusiasm of my girls? I was forced to make a choice. So, I said:

"We shall have to tie some string around the rim of the jars so that you can carry them safely." Their faces radiated joy.

Grampy said:

"Don't be lookin' to use m' garden raffia for this foolhardy skit, I want's nought to do wi' it. We shall end up with a plague of frogs."

We took the jars into the kitchen and used my best parcel string, making a loop for carrying. Soon the other children returned and off they all went on their expedition. How I envied them and rejoiced at their simple pleasures.

By the time Diana and Mary returned with their prized frogspawn, Grampy had relented. He came down the garden path and said:

"Look'e 'ere me ducks, I found this 'ere ol' copper lining, I can prop it up on a couple of bricks and it'll 'old water alright."

I beamed at him as my heart melted, and I said:

"Isn't that lovely! Let's get a pail of water and help the girls pour in their frogspawn."

The girls were delighted as the spawn oozed into the copper and we stood back and admired the results of their adventure.

So it was that the frogspawn lived in the old copper, underneath the rabbit hutches behind the shed. Every morning after breakfast Diana and Mary went round to inspect the spawn and I would often go with them. As the days went on, we marvelled as the spawn grew eyes and arms, then legs and tails. They had become a wriggling mass of tadpoles.

A few days later, disaster struck. The tadpoles were not in the copper, they had been emptied out onto the garden. They were all dead.

Oh the tears! Oh the incomprehension!

I knew immediately it was Grampy's work. I also knew it was my turn to explain the reality of the situation, I needed to be kind but emphatic. I gathered the girls in my arms, and tried my best to explain:

"Grampy was right all along. We haven't got a pond, neither do any of our neighbours, there's nowhere near here for the frogs to live."

Diana and Mary sobbed:

"But we wanted them to turn into frogs." I dried their tears.

"Yes, I know, but they would've died anyway. There were so many of them, they couldn't all live in the copper. Sometimes it's necessary to be cruel to be kind."

Eventually the girls went off to seek their friends and find out what had happened to the other frogspawn from that March day.

That evening when the girls were in bed and the three of us were sitting round the fire, we told Pete about the drama with the frogspawn. When we reached the point where Grampy emptied the emerging froglets onto the garden, he had the final word:

"Well any'ow, what'd we 'ave done with a plague of frogs?"

5

Everything Came to the House

When, in 1945, our parents bought Finchers, Primrose Hill, Widmer End near High Wycombe, they knew it was isolated. Our father only had a motorbike for travel to and from work, and so arrangements were made for essential supplies, most of which were "on the ration", to be delivered.

We became accustomed to a regular procession of callers to the house, whose visits to our back door, as the seasons came and went, marked the time and days of the week.

Often before breakfast the first caller was Doris our paper girl, who our mother would say was "a bit simple". Doris was in her mid-twenties; she was short and round with bobbed dull hair, usually covered with a brown beret pulled well down. In winter she wore a thick tweed coat belted at the waist and in summer a gaberdine mackintosh similarly belted round the middle. Her outfit was completed with thick lisle stockings and brown lace-up shoes. She always had a smile:

"Mornin', 'ere be the paper."

Doris lived with her sister Mabel, at Hazlemere, and as they were distant relatives, Mum would ask:

"Morning Doris, how's Mabel today?"

Doris would reply:

"Keepin' well, thankee," followed by another big grin.

Our paper order kept Doris's satchel full; we took *The Daily Sketch*, (one of the first tabloid newspapers), accompanied on other days, by The *Bucks Free Press*, *The Smallholder* for Dad and Grampy, *Women's*

Weekly for Mum and *Picture Post* on Saturdays. As we grew older, she delivered *Girl* and *School Friend* comics, which my sister and I eagerly awaited and devoured on Wednesdays before school, if possible. On Sundays we took the sensational *News of the World* until Mary and I started school and learnt to read, then it was deemed "unsuitable" and the Sunday paper changed to *The Observer*.

Doris's paper round was on her way to her main work at Stephens' farm at the top of Primrose Hill where she was housemaid to Mrs. Stephens, the farmer's wife.

Not long after Doris, our next visitor could be glimpsed coming past the kitchen window and we heard the familiar clink of milk bottles. It was Leslie Stephens, the young, go-ahead son from Stephens' Farm. He left the milk on our doorstep but never came in because he had been up since dawn, milking his cows, and was wearing a waterproof jacket and wellington boots. He sold most of his milk to a dairy where it could be pasteurised; but he kept enough back to bottle and run his own milk round.

Our order was always the same, a pint per person per day to comply with the milk ration. This came in 3 bottles: 2 quarts and 1 pint (a quart measures two pints; the quart bottles were quite squat, only slightly taller than the pint bottle and all the bottles were sealed with a cardboard disc. We sometimes saved these discs to thread knitting wool through and make into pompoms). The milk was from Jersey cows and the cream on the top was thick and delicious. It was a highlight of breakfast to get cream on our cornflakes or porridge. Milk did not keep in those days before most people had a refrigerator, so Mum gave us plenty of milk drinks, rice puddings, custard, junket, and macaroni cheese.

Leslie's keen business sense and outgoing manner made it easy for him to pass on a friendly word with all his customers:

"Morning Mrs. Farmbrough, everything well?" and Mum would reply perhaps with an update on our childhood ailments:

"Mary's got a nasty cough, so I'm keeping her indoors today."

Later in the day we would see Leslie driving his green Fordson tractor, such a dashing young man! Leslie was part of the farming revolution that, in the ten years we lived on Primrose Hill, turned harvest time on its head. The original method of harvesting a field of wheat into sheaves then standing them in stooks, transporting all back to the farm to make a hayrick for threshing in the winter, gave way to mechanical reaping which separated the grain and created oblong bales of straw that were built into ricks for use when needed; threshing of the grain (to remove the husk) getting underway immediately the crop was off the field.

Breakfast would be long over and washed up before Joan, our post girl arrived. Like Doris, her round started from the Post Office at Hazlemere, but unlike Doris, the route wound round many different roads before arriving at Primrose Hill. Joan always came in her Post Office uniform: blue trousers and jacket with red piping and a fetching cap to match. She rode a Post Office bike, with her postbag on the front tray. She had bouncy blonde curly hair, rosy cheeks, and red lipstick. Joan treated Mum like a long-lost friend, and she was bubbling over with her adventures and dramas:

"You'll never believe… So, I said to him… Would you credit it?" Then in a flash, "Well, can't stand here gossiping all day, TTFN."

Our grocers were Colins and Baker in Desborough Road, on the far side of High Wycombe. On the rare occasions we visited the shop, we would find behind the counter: Mr. Colins, the smaller of the two with grey curly hair, and Mr. Baker, taller, rounder with dark hair, both wearing their proprietorial white coats. They were assisted in the shop by two young men and a girl. Mum would be offered a seat on a tall bent wooden chair alongside the counter and one look from our mother ensured we understood we "must not touch anything". As far as my sister and I were concerned a visit to the shop was always memorable. The distinctive smells of the smoked bacon hanging from the ceiling and the selection of cheeses, mingled with the myriad other fragrances from open goods on display behind the counter. We would watch as the bacon was secured to the slicing machine, a handle turned, and out came a rasher of bacon. Likewise, a huge piece of cheese placed with precision on the marble slab was divided into exact weights by a wire with a cork handle. If we were lucky, we would be offered a small sliver taster of cheese.

Mr Kneen (he told us the K was silent) was our weekly connection to this emporium. His visits to Finchers were on Monday afternoons at half past four. By this time of day Mum would be washed and changed into her afternoon clothes and most likely sewing. Mr. Kneen, wearing his grey delivery driver's coat and fingerless grey knitted gloves, would come into the kitchen and place on the table a cardboard box containing our order.

Mum would check off the list in the grocery book as we helped her empty the box. There were small blue bags folded over at the top containing sugar, currants, raisins, or sultanas, double greaseproof paper with butter folded inside, the same for cheese and lard. Flour came in its own millers' bag, Lyons Tea in quarter pound rectangular packets with collectable tea cards between the wrappers; there would also be a couple of jars of fish paste, a tin of fruit, a small bottle of junket or tin of custard powder. Everything was securely packed without a scrap of plastic or Sellotape – not yet in common usage.

Mr. Kneen was a kindly but matter-of-fact sort of man; he stuck to his job, making sure the business was completed satisfactorily and the cash safely in his leather satchel, together with next week's order book. It was only then he could relax enough to tell Mum about the latest outing in his car.

"The wife and I went over to the Vale of the White Horse on Sunday. Good run, not much traffic. It's only just the other side of Oxford."

"Really," said Mum, lapping it up. "What did you do when you got there?"

"We had a bit of a walk and took a flask of tea. We were back home before dark. Lovely part of the world."

This was before we had a car of our own, and our outings were restricted to walking to visit nearby relations. After Dad bought his first car, Mum would press Mr. Kneen for more precise details of routes to interesting places – these she would store in her memory for our family outings.

We had a delivery every Saturday morning from Potts and Ward, our butchers from Terriers (the village between Hazlemere and High Wycombe). For some incomprehensible reason we were tied to them. They never kept a regular delivery driver and Dad was always complaining about the quality of their meat. Our order was usually a joint of beef for Sunday and a pound of sausage meat and offal for Saturday. Because we kept chickens and rabbits, one of them would occasionally supplement our diet and, of course, we had our own supply of eggs.

Mr Perkins would come to the back door on Tuesday and Friday afternoons with a large flat basket of bread. He worked for Drews the bakers at Terriers. The owner, who was a distant cousin of our mother, would be her baker for the rest of her life. Mum selected our loaves, two large white and one Hovis, and paid Mr Perkins, who always seemed uncomfortable and awkward. He may have been one of the many demobbed servicemen who found it hard to settle after the war, and that their 'hero's return' fell sadly short of expectations.

Mr. Langstone was a greengrocer who called unsolicited on Wednesdays and doubled up on Sundays to sell ice cream. He came round with a horse and cart, stopped outside people's houses and rang a hand bell. His greengrocery was less than fresh, but Mum would buy oranges or any vegetables no longer cropping in our garden. Missing anything essential meant either going without or carrying a heavy load a long way. On Sundays, if we were within hearing distance, Mary and I would respond to his hand bell and clamour for an ice cream, but not always successfully – it had usually started melting anyway.

Our parents were, what nowadays would be called "early adopters", and a washing machine became part of our lives soon after Dad started working at Hoover in 1950. Until that time washing was done with a boiler and mangle, a long, drawn-out affair on Mondays. Tuesday was for ironing. For the first five years at Finchers our sheets were collected once a fortnight by The Royal Bucks Laundry. The laundry provided a long hard rectangular brown waterproof box with attached straps to keep the laundry clean. Mum made entries on the top copy of the duplicate carbon book and the soiled sheets were sent off. The returned clean sheets were checked off on the duplicate copy in the book. When considering the advantage of buying a washing machine, the cost of the laundry was considered "very high" and the acquisition of the washing machine "a very good thing, it would pay for itself".

There were peripatetic callers to the house, Mum usually gave short shrift to the rag-and-bone men but would try to find things that needed sharpening when the knife grinder called.

One irregular but very welcome visitor was Nancy the hairdresser. She would come for the afternoon to perm Mum's hair, and in between processes, cut my sister's and my hair. Nancy was kind and friendly; she wore smart clothes underneath her hairdresser's overalls. Mary and I did not take kindly to anything affecting our hair and no doubt Nancy heard at length about our hair washing dramas on Friday evenings.

We would only let Dad wash our hair with Drene yellow shampoo, and even then, the slightest drop of soap in our eyes brought forth howls. Once the washing was completed, there was a long wait in front of the kitchen fire while our hair dried. Our delayed bedtime made us grumpy and tearful. Nancy came up with a solution. Through her contacts she could get a "Supreme" electric hairdryer: just plug it in and blow it over the hair, and we would be in bed in no time. And that was how in 1948, we became the first family on Primrose Hill to have an electric hairdryer.

6

Our Dad – Pete's Story

6.1 Hazlemere crossroads, Flint Cottage on the left.

Peter Frederick Farmbrough was born at Hazlemere near High Wycombe on April 19th, 1920, in the family home, Flint Cottage, by Hazlemere Crossroads. Pete and his twin sister Pauline were eighth and ninth in a family of ten children, three boys and seven girls.

Their parents, Charlie and Sarah Ellen, were industrious and careful enough to set aside sufficient money after the Great War to buy a plot of land and build their own house only a few hundred yards from Flint Cottage. They called the bungalow The Coppice; it

6.2 Birth of Farmbrough twins, April 1920
Back: Marj, Phyl, Win, Charlie, Jack, Ruby, David
Front: Sarah Ellen with twins on her lap and Connie

had a large kitchen, scullery, larder, washroom, three bedrooms and a front room for visitors. Outside there was a lavatory, a well to collect rainwater and a large garden protected on the northern side where it nestled against a wood.

One day in May 1932, when Pete was just twelve years old, he returned home from school and noticed straw spread across the road outside the house.

"What's all that straw doing in the road?" he asked his sister Ruby.

"Mum's got a terrible headache; she can't bear the sound of the traffic so the straw is to soften the sound from the wheels outside."

Their mother had meningitis and died soon after. It was an unexpected blow for the whole family. Ruby (then aged 19) helped take over the running of the home thus keeping together the family unit – and ties that were to prove enduring for the rest of their lives. At Hazlemere the family were surrounded with good neighbours who provided kindness and practical assistance. Mr Hearne, the coalman, and his wife lived just up the road – she would send a fruit pie down to The Coppice – and Mr Hearne said to Pete:

6.3 Pete with dog Toby, and his father, Charlie

"I'm taking the lorry over to Great Missenden tomorrow to fill up from my coal wagon there, why don't you come with me for the ride?"

To twelve-year-old Pete, Great Missenden sounded like a world away, and he leapt at the chance.

During the 1930's depression, the Farmbrough children were unaware that times were hard, but often their father was on short time, which was common in the furniture trade. On one occasion, when their parents were away for the day, David shot a squirrel, which they prepared and ate:

"Quite tasty too," was the family's response.

6.4 Dog Toby, Pete and Pauline

Many of Pete's interests began during his teens: His fascination with motorbikes began when he taught himself the workings of an internal combustion engine by saving articles from *The Motor Cycle* magazine; and then his cousin Chris Mines made Pete an offer he couldn't refuse:

"On Saturday, why don't you come over and we'll strip down my BSA, clean the points, and you can help me reassemble it."

At the end of the day Pete said to Chris:

"Well, it all makes sense now that I've actually done it. I can't thank you enough, it's been great!"

Chris replied:

"You're a quick learner, once you get a bike of your own, you'll be made!"

On another occasion his brother-in-law, Bert Kilroy, said:

"That Jack Cobb is racing at Brooklands next weekend, do you fancy coming along with me?" Pete had been following his hero in the newspaper and said:

"If he's driving the Napier Railton, perhaps he'll go for the lap record?"

"Yea, wouldn't it be something to see that?" agreed Bert.

Brooklands was the banked motor racing circuit near Weybridge, and Pete's visits there were something he never forgot.

His love of music stemmed from growing up in a family who could all play the piano and sing. Pete joined the Hazlemere Brass Band at

6.5 Hazlemere Brass Band at the Coronation Parade, 1937

an early age and played the tenor horn. His cousin Chris Mines was conductor, his brother-in-law Tom Barker, assistant conductor – both Chris and Tom played cornet. His brother Jack played trombone and his father was a trustee. The band was a village institution, playing regularly at village events, fetes, parades and garden parties. When the band travelled to band contests by coach, Chris Mines would find a suitable spot on the way for them to get out and rehearse, afterwards, memorably saying:

"Time to let out your water lads!"

In 1934 at the age of 14, Pete and his father signed a seven-year apprenticeship agreement. Pete would be trained as a precision engineer at Broom & Wade in High Wycombe (makers of compressed air generators) on a wage of ten shillings for a 48-hour week. His brother Jack had been apprenticed at the same firm. His father, knowing that it was a big step for a young lad, said to Pete:

"You'll have a skill that will last your working life and being in engineering should give you the chance of regular work, which is the devil in the furniture trade."

Four years later, on his daily motorbike ride to and from work, Pete had his eye on Sybil, a young girl living in Terriers, the next village. But being a shy young man, it took a long time for him to pluck up courage to ask to walk her home from church. He was 18, she was 17.

Pete discovered that Sybil was no stranger to tragedy; she had been orphaned by the time she was 4 and after the death of her Granny when she was ten years old, her nearest living relation was her Grampy,

6.6 Sybil in Hughenden Park, 1939

Edmund Rackstraw. Sybil and Edmund were devoted to each other. Sybil worked as a trainee embroideress with a local firm of "out workers", which embellished parts of garments destined for London fashion houses.

As their relationship grew, Pete and Sybil immersed themselves in the activities of the church, becoming Sunday School teachers, and members of the Church Fellowship. The Rev. Leon Mackney, the then vicar of Hazlemere, writing to them 20 years later, said:

> It is difficult to recall the deep voiced slim, somewhat shy young man of those years and his lady love, but the recalling is worthwhile, for at a time when many were lax, you were straight... It reminds me of happy days when you both served under me so very loyally and unobtrusively.

As Pete was coming to the end of his long apprenticeship, knowing he would then start earning a full wage, he said to Sybil:

"I know I'm on a low wage now, so I don't have much to offer you for the time being."

"I don't mind not having money to spend, I just enjoy being with you and all the things we do together," she replied.

Then Pete gathered his courage:

"When I finish my apprenticeship, I'll start to earn more. How would you feel if at that time we got engaged to be married?"

"You know I really want to be with you, but…" Sybil was disconcerted, she wanted a future with Pete, but couldn't bear to be parted from her Grampy.

So, Pete pressed his suit further:

"Once we're engaged, then we could save up to buy a piece of land and build our own home. Grampy could live with us and help with the land."

"That would be wonderful and just what I want, as long as there's a place for Grampy as well." Sybil had the reassurance she sought; she and Grampy had faced the world together since she was ten years old.

For Pete and Sybil their future with Grampy was sealed, and every penny went towards achieving this ambition.

In the meantime, for entertainment at minimum cost, they went by motorbike to Amersham Playhouse, a repertory theatre founded by Sally Latimer, an actor and director, who, by 1938, shared the running with Caryl Jenner. On Monday nights, the offer of two seats for the price of one made it possible for Pete and Sybil to enjoy the latest theatre productions and become familiar with the names and faces of young actors, such as Derek Bogarerd (later Dirk Bogarde), Jill Bennett, Denholm Elliott, Peter Jones, Mary Wimbush, Peter Sallis, Anna Wing and Patrick Troughton.

It gave Pete and Sybil great pleasure, in later years, to see these same actors go on to become household names with careers in film and television.

"Just look at that, there's Kay Kendall, we last saw her at Amersham Playhouse, I'd wondered what'd happened to her."

"Yes, fancy seeing her here in our living room."

When the Second World War was declared, most businesses and industries quickly changed their output to "war work". Broom & Wade started making Churchill tanks and Pete's work was declared a "reserved occupation" which exempted him from military service, but also meant working 60 hours a week in shifts, with no paid holidays. No one thought the war would last for six years but by the end, Broom & Wade had produced more than 3,000 Churchill tanks.

The dexterity of Sybil's colleagues was also harnessed for "war work" and they became involved in making electrical engineering components. Sybil and her workmates learnt to become "armature winders". These windings, usually made of copper, create electromotive force, and the armature converts this to mechanical power.

As the epic drama of the Second World War was unfolding around them, Pete and Sybil kept their dream alive. The War rolled on and took its toll, not just in human lives lost, but also in the accompanying devastation and uncertainty. At home there were severe shortages of every commodity and rationing was introduced: housewives were obliged to join long queues in the shops for scarce supplies.

Pete's employers, Broom & Wade, were allowed to provide a hot canteen meal for each shift to ensure the workers received the minimum

6.7 Pete and Sybil's wedding
Grampy Farmbrough, David, Pete, Sybil, Uncle Will, Aunty Evie, Grampy Rackstraw.

nourishment, but he couldn't get his sister to leave a hot meal for him when he came home at the end of his shift. Sybil convinced him that she could do better; they became engaged on completion of his apprenticeship and a few months later on 25 April 1942, they were married.

After their marriage, Pete and Sybil set up home with Grampy, and for the next three years they were "living in rooms" in Hazlemere, waiting for the war to end.

One evening Pete greeted Sybil with some news: "Ruby says the plot of land next to them is up for sale with planning permission on it."

"Wouldn't it be lovely to live at Widmer End, next to Ruby and Tom? Do you think we have enough saved up to buy the land outright?" Sybil was enthusiastic, she could imagine their dream home. Pete squeezed her hand:

"Yes, and we could go on saving to pay for building our house."

The plot was about half an acre of flat land stretching back from the road towards the east. Living next to Ruby would be so reassuring: she was an accomplished homemaker, and both kind and funny. Tom, who was abroad in the Army during the war, was tall and handsome, well liked and easy to get on with; a key member of the Hazlemere Brass Band and also a motorbike enthusiast.

They called their land the "allotment" and used it for growing fruit and vegetables. Grampy, eighty years old, was keen to help:

"We'll start with a good crop of spuds off the land. I'll chit a few and set 'em as a main crop."

They understood, since the outbreak of the war, that the shortage of manpower (conscripted for National Service) and materials meant all house-building work was abandoned in favour of airfields, armaments factories and military bases, so they knew their dream home wouldn't be possible for a while. What they hadn't reckoned on was that the war would go on for so long. During the war there were a record number of marriages and a huge loss of homes damaged by enemy action, continually increasing the demand for housing. They had no way of knowing that the first priority after the war would be to build prefabricated homes to replace those lost to enemy bombing and also provision for key workers who could help the country recover. Their dream of building a home of their own would be put on hold indefinitely because of government controls.

Whenever his shift work permitted, Pete took part in the local Home Guard defence activities. He particularly enjoyed the outdoor exercises; however, he found the organisation perplexing and amusing. On a night-time patrol, his troop were to install telephone communications down the side of a valley, using cocoa tins and string in place of telephones and wire. He always had a good laugh at the TV programme *Dad's Army*, which, to him, encapsulated his experiences.

"You can't help laughing, it's as though the script writer was listening in to our exercises. It's pathetic really to think the defence of the country relied on a few bits of string and guns without ammunition."

The birth of Diana in 1944 took place at the private Sefton Nursing Home, High Wycombe, and Miss Norburn-Reeve (Matron) signed a receipt for £9.3.0d in respect of nursing home fees.

At the start of 1945, with one daughter and another on the way, and still living in rooms, Pete was forced to reassess their situation:

"We can't let this housing shortage get the better of us, things can't go on like this much longer."

"We should try to get a mortgage," said Sybil, practical as ever. "Then we could buy the bungalow next to Fred Saunders, at Primrose Hill. I hear the wife has been left on her own and she wants to move away."

They moved into Finchers, Primrose Hill, Widmer End during the spring of 1945. The war in Europe ended in August that year. Knowing that Pete could be called up for National Service at any time, they worked at putting the bungalow and garden in good order.

Mary's birth in November 1945 was at the same nursing home, but this time the fees were £17.19.0d including laundry. All was not well with Mary, she developed bronchitis, and when Pete's call-up papers for service in the Navy came, he applied for, and was granted, a deferral because of Mary's condition. The call up came again in the spring, this time to the Army. Pete agreed with Grampy to leave the allotment fallow; and having sold his motorbike, he set off on a snowy March day for Colchester Barracks.

Letter to Sybil: (March 1946)
from No.14140303 Pte Farmbrough (Pete wrote home in pencil):

4 Platoon E Company 67 PTW Meeanee Barracks, Colchester

My dearest Sybil... Well I suppose you would like to know how I've got on today so here goes. When I got down Primrose Hill a little way someone gave me a whistle, when I looked round it was old Tilley. He told me he was just going to work and he's been demobbed 2 weeks. So, I walked to Cosy* with him... He said that he went to Colchester when he joined up and if I could, to get a top tier bunk as far from the door as possible - Anyway

---

*   *Cosy Corner, the nearest stop for buses to High Wycombe.*

that's where the Pte in charge put me so I'm alright, near the fire too...

... There was hardly a trace of snow after I left Wycombe although many fields were water-logged, I should think Widmer End had the heaviest snowfall anywhere.

... Remember me to Grampy, will close now with all my love to you and Diana and Mary. Yours my dearest love, Pete xxx

Then tragedy struck:

TELEGRAM: MRS PETER FARMBROUGH FINCHERS PRIMROSE HILL WIDMER END HIGH WYCOMBE

NO 14140303 PTE FARMBROUGH GRAVELY ILL COLCHESTER MILITARY HOSPITAL STOP NEXT OF KIN ADVISED ATTEND SOONEST

Sybil, in a state of shock, arranged for Ruby to look after 4-month-old Mary, and went by train to Colchester and took Diana with her. She found Pete ill with "double pneumonia" and "his face as grey as the army blanket on his bed". She stayed with Aunt Nell, Grampy Farmbrough's sister. She was landlady of *The Railway Tavern* at Marks Tey just outside Colchester, so Sybil could visit Pete daily.

A picture emerged of what had occurred. Part of the Army six-week initial training included regular cross-country runs. Pete had started to feel unwell and said to the Sergeant Major:

"I need to report to the medical officer, I'm feeling very ill."

Only to be told:

"I've heard that one before, get off on that course and we will see about your complaint when you get back."

Pete was found collapsed and unconscious halfway round the cross-country route and taken straight to the hospital. He did not respond to conventional treatment and was to spend the next four months in Colchester Military Hospital.

Cutting from *Bucks Free Press*, April 1945:

YOUR PRAYERS ARE ASKED... For Diana and Mary's Daddy, gravely ill in a military hospital...

The situation became very tense; Sybil was able to visit the hospital at least once more during April. There is a long gap in the letters from Pete.

(May 1946)

> Dearest Sybil... I have just been told I'm to have my bronchial gram tomorrow afternoon...
>
> ... I'm still wondering how much the sister knows about my future, it would be nice, so long as I feel well, if I came home for good in a few weeks' time wouldn't it. I expect a lot will depend on what they find out tomorrow from the "radio gram".
>
> ... I should think that since I've been in here I've seen close on one hundred patients go out, some only stop two or three days, others a few weeks. I really can't seem to estimate how much longer I shall be here. I wish I could feel a bit better, but I hope they will know what treatment to give me after tomorrow. Don't worry my darling, when I come home I shall be 100% fit and will be happy to work for you and repay you for all you have done for me, your company and love will always keep me going.
>
> ...I don't know how long I'm supposed to be up for now I think its two hours officially, but I usually get up about one o'clock and stay up until about six o'clock. All my love to you. Yours as ever Pete xxx

Sometimes, in spite of his illness, he was able to see the funny side of things (two days later):

> My Dearest Sybil...Well I had a very peculiar sensation yesterday as you know I was to have the bronchial gram...

The sister gave me a little yellow tablet and told me I may see double. Then the fun started. I was jumping up on the bed trying to stand on my head, talking a lot of nonsense and laughing. I was completely out of control...The nurse and sister had to try and hold me down all the afternoon until it wore off. Three MOs came to see me and I made them rock with laughing, the whole ward was roaring with laughter. I've had my leg pulled ever since. The sister gave me some tinned peaches as a consolation prize for the afternoon entertainment... All my love to you, God Bless, Pete xxx

Two days later, Peter is anxious for Sybil to visit Colchester for Whitsun, the "rations" he refers to being coupons from Sybil's personal food ration book:

My Dearest Sybil... I have written to Aunt Nell and asked her if you can come next Friday and stay until Monday (*Whitsun*), is that what you intend doing. I also told her that you would bring a few rations with you...

I haven't had the "gram" yet... they changed their minds yesterday... I expect they will do it tomorrow. You know none of the MOs can look at me now without laughing over Thursday's episode. I laugh myself when I think of it... I shall be glad to have it done now so that I know where I stand. I wish I could see what I am going to do so that I could look forward to something, as it is now I just keep hanging on here and it seems that I have lived in this ward and with this routine for ages. I think that when I do move everything will be strange and it will seem like emerging from a dream.

If everything goes alright this week I should think I could get an afternoon pass next weekend but that will depend on the MOs and they are very careful not to take risks of a relapse, but in any case you could stay with me quite a few hours in here... Yours as always, Pete xxx

By the middle of June 1946, Pete was sufficiently recovered to be allowed home on weekend leave, and afterwards return to Rushbrook, the Army Convalescent Home just south of Bury St Edmunds, for a further two weeks.

First day at Rushbrook:

> Dearest Sybil, I thought I would drop you a line to let you know I have arrived here OK... Well, it's been a nice weekend for me and thank you darling for all you've done for me. I feel much better for being home and when I come home again I shall be OK. I want the next fortnight to seem short... All my love to you, Pete xxx

After a week at Rushbrook:

> My Dearest Sybil... I hope to be on the move next Monday... I don't know quite what to think about rehabilitation as I'm not very keen on leaving home again, but I'll get all the dope from the Commandant and then think it over.
>
> I'm looking forward to getting home and getting busy with the hoe, I must do some work otherwise I shall get too lazy... What a difference there will be to when we first moved in and what a blessing we managed to get the place. This housing shortage seems to hit most service men and we know how hard it hits. I often doubt whether Rothschild was any happier in his mansion than we are in our bungalow... Yours with all my love, Pete xxx

When called up to serve in the Army, the independent Medical Assessment Board had found Pete's health grade B2 (Grade B signified "Unfit for service abroad but fit for base or garrison service at home and abroad"). After his illness, the assessment, conducted in July 1945, found he was suffering from bronchiectasis and he was awarded medical grade E4 (Grade E signified "Permanently unfit"). He had a 30% disability for the rest of his life.

Pete came home with a small disability pension, which, more importantly (because there was no NHS), entitled him to free medical treatment. He brought with him, as rehabilitation therapy, a semi-circular rug tapestry kit, rug wool and 2 hooks available from Rushbrook at a cost of £2.

In the evenings, after putting the children to bed, they sat round the fire, with Grampy nodding in his Windsor chair. Together at last, Pete and Sybil took out the tapestry rug kit and started knotting the wool, chatting comfortably as they did so. Pete gently murmured:

"After all we've been through, it's so lovely to be sitting here with you making this rug."

And Sybil whispered:

"There were times when I never dared hope this would happen or that we would ever be together again."

They made a cream semi-circular rug decorated with intertwined pink roses and green leaves and kept this rug at their bedside for many years. Pete slowly grew stronger and returned to work.

The following winter (1946/1947) was the harshest winter of the twentieth century with continuous frost, snow and blizzards lasting from late January to mid-March (for the whole of February the daytime temperature was below freezing). The country was brought to a standstill; coal could not reach power stations causing massive disruption of energy supply for homes, offices and factories; and severe hardship in economic and living conditions. Restrictions on electricity supply only ended in April 1947.

Pete suffered the first of what would prove to be regular relapses necessitating weeks in bed recovering. The scarring on his lungs left him prone to regular chest infections. Over time their plans and ambitions had to be adjusted as they concentrated on what was possible within their evident limitations.

Sybil and Pete remained members of Hazlemere Church for the rest of their lives. The damage to his lungs made it impossible for Pete to play a wind instrument, and he had to give up Hazlemere Brass Band. The land at Widmer End was sold in 1951. The prescription of antibiotics for treatment of Pete's bronchiectasis was introduced in 1957.

Pete and Sybil were married for 56 years, until his death on 23 April 1998.

7

Home Sweet Home – The Front Room

Dad was in the front room making a bookcase. We heard banging and smelt sawdust; my sister Mary and I lingered in the hallway trying to catch a glimpse of what was going on. We knew better than to get under his feet because Dad was huffing and puffing.

"Mum says we need a bookcase," I told Mary.

"What do you think it will look like?" she asked.

The new bookcase would fill the alcove next to the fireplace on the right-hand side. The room had two windows, the bay window opposite the door and another south-facing window on the left; sunlight streamed through these two windows and made the room bright and airy. However, in the winter, it took a long time to warm up even with a blazing fire. On the floor was a square brown Axminster carpet with an abstract yellow and blue design; beyond the carpet the floorboards were dark stained. Other furniture included a utility dining table, four chairs with cold-to-sit-on Rexine-covered seats, a sideboard, and four easy chairs.

In years to come, this room would evoke many happy memories. Of birthday and Christmas parties, playing games like *Pin the Tail on the Donkey* and *Squeak Piggy Squeak*; for Mary's November birthday, there were often indoor fireworks. Memories of Sunday afternoon teas followed by card games like *Snap*, *Happy Families*, or *Lexicon* (a forerunner of *Scrabble*) and board games like *Snakes & Ladders*, *Tiddly Winks*, and *Ludo* all fiercely contested, with Mum and Dad taking one of us on to their side. The television, with a tiny nine-inch screen, was bought in time for the Coronation of Queen Elizabeth II, and most of our neighbours at Primrose Hill came to watch.

The front room was also full of benign ghosts from our mother's past. Some lived on the mantelpiece and took the form of porcelain Welsh Ladies sat at a small table taking tea; and a pair of gold and white Staffordshire china dogs won by Grampy at Penn Fair. In the sideboard there was a bone china tea service and a set of Georgian wine glasses. These ghosts came from the home where our mother grew up, until she was ten. With the death of Granny in 1931 these few possessions were stored in a tea chest until our parents bought Finchers in 1945 and brought them back to everyday use. Mary and I knew that we touched them at our peril.

For some years Mary and I slept in the front room, sharing a divan (sleeping top and bottom), starting from the spring of 1946. I was nearly two years old and Mary only 6 months when, in May 1946, Dad wrote a letter home from the military hospital:

> Fancy the children sleeping on their own. I think it's a good idea during the summer specially; and in the winter if its not too cold. Can you imagine the happiness next Christmas morning of those two, we will try and make them happy always...

The divan we shared was covered with a tailored fitted cover made of thick but soft sateen with a cream background and green and brown leaf pattern and this cover made the room "presentable" for use when visitors came.

Everything changed after Grampy died in February 1951. Mary and I moved into Grampy's bedroom. The front room furniture was rearranged and walls redecorated with cream wallpaper, which was hazardous when touched because the gold and red swirl pattern came off on our hands and clothes.

Book storage had become a problem. Mum was an avid reader and, in addition to the three books she always brought home from the library in High Wycombe every two weeks, she had joined "The Companion Book Club" and a new book arrived in the post every month. Piles of books had grown on our parent's bedroom floor. Dad wanted to build the bookcase for Mum because he knew how much her books meant to her.

Dad stood back to assess his progress with the bookcase:

"None of these walls are square. How are you expected to get a shelf to fit?" he grumbled.

Mum brought a cup of tea to cheer him on, and commented:

"Well, I know you are a precision engineer and can make anything in metal, but woodworking isn't one of your strengths."

7.1 Diana and Mary, Christmas 1947

When it was finished, the bookcase looked superb. It fitted the alcove precisely and rested on top of the deep wainscot. It had an intricate plaited reed beading fixed along the front of the shelves.

"This is just what I wanted, now my books can be set out properly. They will look lovely, just like our own library."

"I'm glad you're pleased. It'll be good to clear the bedroom floor and get this front room straight," said Dad.

Mum was delighted to arrange her books. Some of them would stay with her for the rest of her life. Authors like Neville Shute and *A Town Like Alice*, Monica Dickens *One Pair of Hands* and Nicholas Monserrat *The Cruel Sea*. Dad had a shelf with a set of books called *The Great War in Pictures* described as the standard history of the All-Europe Conflict – very boring for children. Mary and I started building up our own collection of the *Swallows & Amazons* series, and other favourites like *Black Beauty*, *The Secret Garden* and *The Wind in the Willows*. The lowest and deepest shelf was eventually occupied by Arthur Mee's *The Children's Encyclopaedia*, in ten volumes.

There would be many cold wet days when this collection of books occupied my sister and me. We would sit cross-legged on the floor poring over our book of choice.

David, our bachelor uncle, made a wooden octagonal birdcage. It was a gift to Mary and me and it just fitted on top of the bookcase. The front three sides were fitted with a metal grill with a sliding door in the middle. Inside the cage was a lovely green budgerigar and we called him Joey.

I was so proud and happy to be given the task of refilling Joey's seed and water and to pull out the sliding tray at the bottom and change the bird sandpaper floor covering. Inside the cage there was a cuttlefish for his beak, a spray of millet and a toy mirror with a bell. I had been taught how to hold him properly, and sometimes Joey would perch on my finger when my hand was in the cage. Dad would meet us after Saturday morning pictures at the Odeon, then we went to Jones & Rivett, the corn and seed merchants, to buy supplies for Joey, as well as for our hens.

One day when we were a bit bored, Mary and I decided we would teach Joey to talk; we wanted him to say:

"Watcha, who's a pretty boy then?"

We would speak these words every time we entered the front room, and at any opportune moment whilst we were there; but try as we might, after more than a year, he only whistled and chirped back.

The inevitable day came when Joey did not respond when we entered the front room, his little body lay still on the cage floor.

"Mum, something terrible has happened to Joey. We think he's dead."

"Let's have a look at him," said Mum, coming into the room. "Oh, dear, poor little thing, I think you're right." Mum dried our tears, and continued:

"Of course, we didn't know how old he was when he came to us, and this is what happens to poor little animals, they don't live as long as we humans do."

We were not ready to be consoled: "But we didn't have time to teach him to talk to us."

Mum reassured us:

"I know, but he did have a good and happy life with us. He was well cared for, so we mustn't be too sad for him."

Mum went to the sideboard cupboard and took out a box of

Newberry Fruits, emptied the sweets into a teacup and brought the box to us standing by the cage. She placed Joey's body inside and covered it with the plush inside wrappers.

"We must give him a proper funeral and show respect for the happiness he gave us."

We followed Mum to the back garden where she dug a deep hole under a blackcurrant bush and we put the precious box in the hole. As Mum refilled the hole, we clasped our hands together and said our prayers.

A precedent had been set, any future budgie deaths were ceremoniously dispatched in a sweet box from the sideboard, sometimes a marshmallow box (our mother's favourites), or Maltesers, or Batger's Silmos Lollies.

Just down Primrose Hill, on the opposite side to us, lived Fred and Perse White. Mary and I thought Mrs. White's name was "Purse" and we wondered:

"Where does she keep the money?"

Dad laughed, and told us her name was Persephone, Perse for short. Mr and Mrs White were Welsh, middle-aged with no children living at home, and like many couples, had grown alike: short, round and with dark hair. Mr. White was a Special Constable; Mary and I were in awe:

"So you've come to look at our aviary have you?" said Mr. White.

"We are so sorry you have lost Joey, perhaps you will find another budgie you like here," said Mrs. White.

Mary and I were not sure what an aviary was, but we heard the birds chattering and fluttering before we turned the corner of their bungalow. We were captivated with such a happy sight of a large walk-in aviary: there were budgerigars of all shades of blue and green flying around naturally, some sat on small tree branches grooming each other. They had swings, nest boxes and a birdhouse for the night.

"Budgies like to live in a flock and are lonely on their own," explained Mr. White as he opened the aviary door and hung a fresh spray of millet from one of the twigs.

"Which colour budgie do you like best?" asked Mrs. White.

That was how we came home with two budgies, one green and one blue. We called the green one Joey No.2 and the blue one Bluey. After that we gave up trying to teach the budgies to talk. When the weather was bad, we were content to sit on the floor in the front room reading our books and listen to the budgies chattering away above us in their octagonal home, with occasional husks of seed dropping on our heads.

The front room at Finchers was not just for best, it was where we did special things. Having beautiful budgerigars living on top of the bookcase made it even more special. The room was so full of happy memories, possibly even the ghosts were happy too.

8

The Orange Juice Tea Party

On a golden April afternoon, the girls open a green plastic doll's tea service from Woolworths. They want to entertain their toys.

A blanket is laid on the front lawn where the grass is long with daisies and dandelions in flower; in the surrounding hedges, birds are chattering.

In anticipation the girls carefully seat their dolls and teddies; their horse on wheels is there and looks on.

Mother dilutes concentrated welfare orange juice with water and sugar and fills the toy teapot.

The girls each dispense drinks to their own dolls and teddies.

They sip orange from the tiny cups; it's bitter: the sugar hasn't dissolved.

They make daisy chains for their toys in the sunshine.

9

Our Dad – The Joy of the Open Road – The New Car

In the late 1940s, as Britain was recovering from the War, our dad, Pete, still a young man in his mid-twenties, was determined to resist the gloom and inertia that pervaded everyday life. With a young family and a medical condition that restricted his physical abilities, he recognised that his motorbike, essential for travel to work each day, was not suitable for family use. He wanted a car of his own.

Dad had been inspired by the Shell Guides to Cornwall, Dorset and Buckinghamshire, copies of which he devoured before the War, and he was eagerly awaiting the golden age of the motor car and the opportunity to become part of it.

In 1948, before his hopes could be fulfilled, the chance of a holiday on the Essex coast came up. The challenge of taking a family of five on a journey of over one hundred miles was resolved by the hire of a taxi from the garage at Hazlemere Crossroads; Dad had been at school with the garage owner's son, Reg, who would chauffeur. There was room in the limousine and the holiday bungalow for two more and so a friend of the family, Mrs. Worcester, and her daughter, Jean, came along as well, to share the cost.

The expedition to Holland-on-Sea in 1948 achieved what holidays are supposed to: long days were spent on the beach, building sandcastles, paddling and sitting in the sun. At the holiday bungalow Mum made good use of the free plums and runner beans in the garden. Mary and I made beds for our dolls in a drawer from the chest of drawers in our bedroom. We developed a taste for shellfish bought for a few pence

9.1 Holland on Sea, 1948. Jean, Mrs Worcester, Sybil, Pete,
Grampy Rackstraw, Diana and Mary

in a paper bag, to which we added vinegar and picked winkles out of
their shells with a pin.

Down by the sea, Dad made friends with a well-known boxer,
Freddie Mills, who was about to become World Light Heavyweight
Champion (1948-1950). Freddie was to be found training on the beach
most days. After we returned home, Dad followed the boxer's career as
he went from strength to strength. Dad's enthusiasm later turned to
intrigue and gradually horror as Freddie Mills became a nightclub owner
and met an untimely death in Soho in 1965. It emerged that Mills had
been a friend of notorious gangland criminals, the Kray twins. Dad's
hero had feet of clay and he was appalled. But all that was in the future.

On the return journey, sitting next to Reg Stacey, Dad said:

"You know, watching you, I think once I've got the hang of the
controls, I could soon learn to drive a car."

Reg laughed, as he changed gear and expertly cruised round a
bend. He agreed:

"You really ought to have a go mate, it's not difficult."

In the back seat Mum's ears pricked up at the talk of having a

9.2 Diana and Mary on the beach.
Holland on Sea, 1948

car of our own, and looking at the passing scenery, she thought of all the places we could visit, and she joined in:

"What a difference a car would make to our lives, and for you getting to work in bad weather, Pete."

Detecting a mood of consensus, Reg continued:

"Once you get your own car, you won't have to go around in taxis anymore. You'd save money there straightaway."

There was a murmur of agreement from the back seat and Pete had another thought:

"I won't have to pay for a driving test either, because the driving licence I have for my motorbike includes cars as well. The trouble is, I've been looking around: new cars are hard to come by and they are kept for people like doctors, and folk are holding on to the pre-war models."

Reg nodded:

"When you're ready, I'll keep an eye out for a car. for you, a good runner and not too expensive."

"I need to make some preparations before I get a car. I don't have a garage or a driveway wide enough to get the car past the house."

At this point Grampy, who'd been listening intently to the conversation, joined in saying:

"Tha' lonicera 'edge at the side of our path is so thick, if you cuts it back, you'd get a car up alright."

Reg laughed again and said:

"Sounds like you'd better get a move on then, Pete. Now I come to think of it, I might know a car that's been laid up on bricks since the start of the War. The husband was killed at Dunkirk, and his widow won't drive. I could have a word with her and see if it's for sale."

Pete was won over; the prospect of owning his own car was irresistible, inspiring, and motivating. The joy of the open road beckoned.

After the holiday, there followed a period of intense preparations, garage building, hedge cutting and driveway concreting. Unfortunately, the clouds of dust from the lonicera hedge caused a flare-up of Dad's chest complaint and he was off work for two weeks with no sick pay. However, once recovered, and undeterred, he continued with his project.

At last, the great day arrived, and the Hillman Minx, AME225, was brought home to Finchers, and there was excitement all round, with Dad keen to inspect the engine under the bonnet, Mum cleaning inside and polishing the leather seats, and Mary and me jumping in and out of the doors and watching the indicator arms as they waved up and down on the left and right.

"You two be careful what you get up to, this car's not a toy," warned Dad.

Being an engineer, Dad soon knew the intimate workings of his new car and dismissed any suggestion of wasting money on joining the AA in case it broke down. Instead, he carried his own tool set under the driver's seat, alongside the starting handle. In those days membership of the AA included a large brass and enamel badge to be fixed to the front radiator of the member's vehicle. The AA repair men were often stationed by the AA Call Boxes ready to respond on their bright yellow motorbike and sidecar (the sidecar contained the repair equipment). The AA men were instructed to salute any vehicle they met bearing the AA Membership Badge.

"We can have a bit of fun," said Dad. "I hate to see my Hazlemere Band Uniform going unused. I think I'll attach the brass hat badge to the car radiator. It will look fine." From a distance it looked just like an AA Members' Badge.

Of course, when out in the car, Mary and I had as much fun looking out for an approaching yellow motorbike and sidecar as Dad did when he returned the AA salute! Mum pretended to be embarrassed and looked the other way.

As they got used to having a car, our parents became increasingly adventurous with picnics by the Thames and at Burnham Beeches, visits

9.3 Pauline, Reg, Sybil, Pete, Mary, Geoffrey and Diana, Westgate-on-Sea, 1949

to family in Wood Green, and Weybridge, and day trips to various seaside locations along the South Coast from Bournemouth to Brighton. In 1949 we went on a camping holiday to Westgate-on-Sea in Kent with Dad's twin sister Pauline, her husband Reg, and our cousin Geoffrey.

By 1950, there were about four million licensed vehicles on the road and the enthusiasm for car ownership was growing. At Primrose Hill, it wasn't long before our neighbour, Pete Saunders, came home with a car of his own.

Seeing Dad admiring his car, Pete Saunders came over to the low hedge next to our driveway and, glowing with pride, he pointed at his new car:

"This 'ere 'Morris Twalve', runs like a dream. I can get over to work at the gravel pits at Marlow in record time."

"It's a smart looking car, and I'm glad it's going well," replied Dad, not a shred of jealousy in his mind.

"I was thinkin' of taking this 'ere car to the coast next weekend, but the *missus* is no good with maps. What'd ya' suggest?"

As it happened Mum and Dad had already made plans, so Dad said:

"We are going down to Hayling Island next Sunday; why don't you follow behind us, and you can learn the way as you go."

That was how the convoy of the Hillman Minx and Morris Twelve set off soon after 6 o'clock on a bright midsummer morning, following a route over Marlow Bridge and through the still asleep towns of Maidenhead, Aldershot and the villages of Bracknell and Petersfield, arriving at Hayling Island in time for breakfast by 9 o'clock. The Saunders car contained Pete, his wife Rose, their daughter Rita, and her uncle Keith; in our car was Dad, Mum, Mary and me. Our Grampy, now in his late eighties, was happy to stay at home and feed the chickens. There was time for a paddle in the freezing sea, shivering in the chilly breeze coming off the water. We made sandcastles and ate our sandwiches on the beach just before the start of the return journey.

9.4 Hayling Island trip – Rose, Pete and Rita Saunders, Pete, Dianna, Keith Pearce and Mary in front.

A 'good day out' had to ensure we would all be home for bedtime and ready for school and work the following day.

To us, Hayling Island was just one of many interesting seaside places where we could spend a nice day, but to Pete Saunders it represented the ultimate travel destination. For the remainder of our time at Primrose Hill, we never heard of him or the 'Morris Twalve' venturing elsewhere other than to '*Ayling Island*'.

To pass the time on long journeys, the whole family would join in singing songs we learnt at school from *The National Song Book*, interspersed with hymns from church. The words and sentiments of these songs reflected the patriotism and values at the time and seemed perfectly normal.

Mum had a lovely, sweet soprano voice and Mary and I tried to follow her pitch. Dad was a deep baritone and he often harmonised with us rather than hold the tune.

One of our favourites was **Heart of Oak,** a rousing and patriotic song about being "free as the sons of the waves". Sometimes after singing this song, Dad would remind us that he was originally called up for National Service in the Navy but had to defer because of Mary's bronchitis. We thought, wistfully, how romantic it would have been if he had served in the Navy.

One of our favourites from church, because we would all let rip for the chorus, was the hymn **Onward Christian Soldiers;** Mum would sometimes sing a plaintive song – **Early One Morning** – which tells the story about a heartbroken young girl watching the sun rise as she sings about being deceived and abandoned by her lover. We would learn the words and tune from her and merrily sing along unconcerned about the story as it was obviously something that happened to other people, and we didn't give too much thought to it. Another song our Mum taught us was:

Dashing Away with a Smoothing Iron
It was on a Monday morning that I beheld my darling,
She looked so neat and charming in every high degree,
She looked so neat and nimble oh!

A washing of her linen oh!
Dashing away with a smoothing iron, she stole my heart away.

Second verse, fourth line: A hanging out her linen oh!
Third verse, fourth line: A bringing in her linen oh!
Fourth verse, fourth line: A folding of her linen oh!
Fifth verse, fourth line: Ironing of her linen oh!

We thought this song was about Mum, and we loved it when Dad sang, "She stole my heart away."

Dad's dream had come true; the Hillman Minx brought untold opportunities for a more meaningful family life, and freedom at last from the constraints of his long apprenticeship, the war years and ill health. The Hillman Minx was his pride and joy. However, after five years, a broken half-shaft proved too expensive to repair, and ushered in the next car, a Morris Eight, CBH 888. This was the car which took us on camping holidays to Wales and eventually to Swanage.

For Dad the joy of the open road never dimmed; he and Mum were always planning their forthcoming trips and holidays. They never

9.5 Camping in Wales, 1953

missed a Good Friday outing to somewhere sacred like Winchester Cathedral, or Stonehenge. On Whit Saturday the arrangement, for years, was to meet Pauline and Reg at Bognor Regis, Bournemouth, or Swanage for a walk round the shops and a picnic lunch in the park – Whitsun usually being too cold for the beach.

It was from these Whitsun trips, when the sun was warm, but the wind decidedly chilly, that Aunty Pauline's regular exclamation became a family mantra:

"It's a hot and cold day."

There was an intuition between Pete and Pauline. Quite often on a Sunday afternoon jaunt to somewhere like Burnham Beeches, he would say:

"I think we'll see Pauline soon."

And low and behold, round the next corner, we would see the Osborne Wolseley car approaching. It was a remarkable affinity.

Dad would have been amazed that in his lifetime something as malevolent as toxic air pollution had occurred from use of the motor car and traffic congestion. He would have found it hard to conceive that a government would propose making payments to drivers to encourage removal of the most polluting cars from the road and substitution with bicycles, electric cars and scooters.

By the time of his death in 1998, he had already lived through the golden age of the motor car.

10

Finding Swanage in 1953

After a touring holiday in Wales where it rained every day, we returned home early to Finchers; but as there were just a few days of Dad's annual holiday left, our parents decided to go away again, but this time to try the south coast. Starting near Bournemouth they spent a whole day searching unsuccessfully for a vacant campsite; eventually, just as the light was fading, they happened upon a camping field at Swanage, in Dorset.

The next day we discovered a picture-postcard location, a sheltered bay with golden sands for safe swimming, shaded gardens behind for our parents to use as a base for picnics. There was an unpretentious shopping centre with a wide range of interesting shops; in the evenings: pitch and putt, band concerts and walks to Durlston or Tilly Whim Caves. Most important, there was a Forte's Ice Cream Parlour for a knickerbocker glory treat on the last day of our family holiday.

We agreed Swanage had something for everyone: unknown to us at the time, after the birth of our sister Hilary, Swanage was to be our family holiday destination for many years to come.

10.1 Mary and Diana in knitted swimsuits at Swanage, 1953

11

Our Mum – Sybil Makes Jams and Preserves

During the Second World War many people devised ways to get round the restrictions of rationing and use of coupons. Pete and I used to save petrol by cycling on our tandem twenty-two miles each way from Hazlemere to Weybridge to visit my "Granny at Weybridge". Her name was Eunice, she was my Granny's niece, and we were very fond of each other. It was a sad day when she died in 1946.

On a visit in 1943, she gave me a cookery book, saying:

"As a young wife setting up home, you need a good recipe book."

And after I thanked her, she continued:

"You'll find the instructions from 'Soups' to 'Fruit Preserving and Pickles' will give you confidence to tackle any challenge that comes your way in the kitchen."

She was right; I kept this book by me all my life.

11.1 Sybil with Granny at Weybridge
(Eunice)

When Pete and I bought Finchers in 1945, the shed was a bit of a glory hole:

"Just look at all this junk," Pete was not impressed.

On investigation, however, I was overjoyed to find a couple of wooden boxes containing Kilner and jam jars, because during the War, these were difficult to come by.

"Isn't that lucky. These will give me a head start when I deal with the fruit from the garden. I only need to buy seals for the jam jars and rubber rings for the preserving jars."

By 1950 I had established a routine for making jams and preserves that followed the seasons and gave me great satisfaction as I filled the shelves in our larder.

"January brings the snow, makes our feet and fingers glow."

Every January, when Seville oranges became more readily available again after the war, I would ask Mr. Langstone, our greengrocer, if he could get some for marmalade because Pete did like marmalade for breakfast. Once I had the oranges, the next challenge was to make sure I had enough sugar (sugar was rationed until 1953). Usually, I could swap something with Eva Saunders, my neighbour, or with one of Pete's sisters.

I always found getting marmalade to set a challenge, and the pages of my Good Housekeeping Cookery Book bear this out, the most heavily splattered being "Three Fruit" and "Orange" Marmalade. Some people found the distinctive, sharp smell of marmalade boiling unpleasant, but the end result made up for this.

It was so pleasing to be making marmalade in our cosy kitchen with frost or snow outside the window and the comforting presence of Grampy, sitting beside me in his Windsor chair. We often had the wireless on and, in the last few months of his life, we did so enjoy listening to *The Archers,* the everyday story of country folk, which had just started. He really liked Dan and Doris Archer who lived at Brookfield Farm and chuckled at Walter Gabriel the village grouch. Throughout my life, listening to *The Archers* has been an invisible link to Grampy and those days.

"March brings breezes loud and shrill, stirs the dancing daffodil."

In the garden there were signs of new growth; our robin, who had been singing outside the backdoor all winter, was joined by the joyful trills of a thrush and blackbird, heralding the spring. Our hens, often replacement pullets, responded to the hint of new life and, clucking companionably to each other, would come into lay; at first their eggs were small, but as the days lengthened, they laid regular-sized eggs and I often got more than two eggs a day per bird, and became inundated.

I experimented with preserving eggs in isinglass, bought from the chemist. I heated the isinglass mixed with water and when it cooled down and became jelly-like, I poured it into a deep bowl and placed clean, uncracked eggs into the mixture. Later, when using these eggs, I always cracked them into a cup first to see if they were still usable because the yolks were often broken, and only good for cake-making or scrambling. So, using isinglass wasn't something I did unless hard-pressed to use up the eggs.

"June brings tulips, lilies, roses, fills the children's hands with posies."

As the spring turned into summer, and the blossoms set to fruit, my thoughts turned to jam-making. There was a strawberry field behind Finchers, cultivated by Mr. Tilbury, a taciturn man. He didn't live at Primrose Hill, so in June I made a point of catching him either when he was coming to or going from his field on his trade bicycle.

"Hello Mr. Tilbury, I wonder whether you can spare a few pounds of strawberries for jam?"

He would tilt the brim of his trilby hat and scratch his head, and always made the same reply:

"I shall 'ave to see 'ow things go. This be a bad year for strawberries."

Over the years I worked out that if the weather was bad, he could lose his crop; if he got a good crop, there could be a glut, and the price would go down so he got a poor return. I would try to look concerned and say:

"Please do your best."

Making strawberry jam filled the kitchen with delicious, sweet, fruity aromas. I always made jam in the afternoons. On the wireless, *Listen with Mother* was followed by *Woman's Hour*. Grampy and I would listen as these programmes gave way to the cricket test match commentary. All the while I stirred the pan and waited for the boiling jam to set. Occasionally Diana and Mary arrived home from school before I was finished:

"Would you like to get changed and go out on your bikes for a while until I can clear the table?"

"Yes, please Mum, we won't go too far."

"Make sure you're back in time for supper."

"Hot July brings cooling showers, apricots, and gillyflowers."

Some of our neighbours had a cherry orchard. Old Mr. Saunders up the road used to make ladders for the cherry harvest. He took the girls and me to see his large workshop behind their house and demonstrated his spoke shaver, sitting the girls on it in turn and laughing when their legs didn't reach the foot control. Cherry ladders were wide at the bottom rung, narrowing towards the top for poking between the branches.

Pete used to say that when he was a boy in Hazlemere, the cherry orchards came right up to the crossroads, and Grampy told me the cherry harvest was a big thing, most of the crop going to London, but with enough left over for cherry pie suppers at the chapel. If I could get a few pounds of cherries in July, I would preserve as much as possible in Kilner jars and make a fresh cherry pie and cherry turnovers for afters.

11.2 Eating cherry turnover

"August brings the sheaves of corn, then the harvest home is borne."

During July and August, the gooseberries, raspberries, red and blackcurrants in our garden would invariably crop all at once and kept me busy preserving what I could and making jam. Preserving fruit was economical on sugar, only a light syrup or even plain water was needed to cover the fruit, but everything had to be sterile and the jars airtight. A great treat at this time of year was summer pudding.

What a delight to see the jam and preserving jars, with their distinctive shades of red and gold, filling up the larder shelf.

"Warm September brings the fruit; sportsmen then begin to shoot."

All too soon, the long warm summer days were fading, there was a nip in the morning air and the nights were drawing in.

At the start of the new school year, Diana and Mary were transformed from grubby urchins with fruit-stained fingers into tidy schoolgirls, and it gave me pleasure to watch them set off to school looking so neat wearing their new gymslips, vyella blouses, ties, cardigans, gaberdine raincoats, berets and lace-up boots.

"Have you got your bus fare and school dinner money safe in your purses?" They both had divided leather purses attached to their satchels.

"Yes Mum, and we've got our savings stamp money as well."

When they returned home from school, I would sometimes ask them:

"Just pop over the road and fill this bowl with blackberries for my suet pudding." The hedge opposite Finchers could be relied on to provide a picking, and the girls would return with a good helping in no time.

September was the time to do some proper blackberrying, and one Sunday towards the middle of September, when the days were still warm and the sky unclouded blue, Pete and I would take the car and meet the girls from Sunday School. We planned to go over to a good place with plentiful sprays of big fat blackberries.

I wanted to save their Sunday best outfits and told them:

"We're going blackberrying, so I've brought play clothes and wellington boots for you to change into."

"Oh Mum, do we have to? We can be really careful."

I was ready with my reply:

"Please don't make a fuss, you won't be happy when you scratch your legs on the brambles, and we all know that you'll be covered in purple blackberry stains in no time."

Once parked at Christmas Common, we each had a jam jar to fill and then emptied them into my lined shopping basket, while Pete set up the Primus stove and windbreak for a cup of tea. Then, when the shopping basket was full, we would sit on a groundsheet in the sun and eat jam sandwiches and a piece of cake and linger until the sun dipped below the treeline. On the way home I would calculate how many pounds of blackberry jelly I could make from our haul of nature's bounty.

The next day being Monday was my busy washing day, so I had to fit cooking and straining the fruit around my other tasks. By the end of the next day, I was pleased to have produced five one-pound jars of blackberry jelly: it was so handy for jam tarts, sponge or suet puddings, stirring into semolina, as well as on bread at teatime, and the jars gave off a lovely luminous purple glow on the larder shelf.

There were other harvest bounties: tomatoes came our way unexpectedly. At the end of the war, our neighbour, Pete Saunders, decided he would take advantage of a government scheme to build a greenhouse and grow tomatoes on the vacant land between our two houses. There were Italian Prisoners of War at Hazlemere Park (The Park), the former manor that had been commandeered during the War for troops. A group of these POWs came and, to everyone's amazement, amid loud laughter and exuberant singing, assembled and glazed the 10ft greenhouse in no time at all.

Each summer after that, Diana or Mary would buy half-a-pound of tomatoes whenever needed, and in addition, at the end of the season, when the plants were stripped, Pete Saunders would send round a bowl of green tomatoes for making chutney.

Autumn is a time for taking stock; it was always comforting to know that I had sufficient preserves to make a fruit pie every weekend and a fruit sponge or suet pudding during the week. Pete and I recalled only too well the freezing winter of 1947 and we felt the responsibility of providing for two small children weigh heavily on us; I would never want to go through another winter like that again.

By the end of October Pete and Grampy would have the garden tidy for the winter. Onions and shallots would be hung in plaited strings in the shed and I would use some of this crop to make pickled onions. The vegetable garden was left with only hardy root crops and Brussels sprouts.

"Dull November brings the blast, then the leaves are falling fast."

The seasons changed, the fiery colours of autumn faded; with the land tidied, Grampy took the opportunity to burn the pea sticks and bean poles while Pete was at work (and my washing was safely out of the way). Pete was suffering badly with his weak chest and the combination of smoke and cold wet nights made him worse, so bonfires were to be avoided. The girls didn't seem to mind; they were glad to join their friends whose families burnt a Guy Fawkes on their bonfire and would come home with tales of ooh! and aah! at the "terrific" fireworks.

"Chill December brings the sleet, blazing fire
and Christmas treat."

The garden was asleep. Grampy or I took a morning walk up the garden to let the hens out and feed them, shutting them up again before it got dark. Life slowed down, our life revolved round the kitchen, as we moved into the dark days before Christmas.

(Lines from The Months by Sara Coleridge, 1802-1852)

12

Grampy Rackstraw Dies

When Dad was working at Hoover's their annual children's party was held in the New Year. Dad took us there one Saturday afternoon in February, and unknown to us, at some time that day, our Grampy Rackstraw died.

At the party we were surprised at how many children there were and how large the factory canteen was; but we were soon caught up in the party because everything was well organised with games, a magician and two clowns performing slapstick jokes. For tea, we were disappointed not to be served with Hoover's speciality: baked Alaska, an American cake covered with ice cream and then cooked, because Dad had told us how amazing it was. But what we were offered was a wide array of sandwiches, cakes, pastries and chocolate treats far beyond any party tea we had, so far, ever experienced.

When Mum and Dad met us from the party, we could tell something was up. Unusually, Mum sat with us on the back seat of the car and she was holding our cat, Nipper; she then started to tell us what had happened:

"You know that Grampy was ill in bed, and Dr. Wilson came to see him, but couldn't make him better. Well, Grampy fell asleep and he didn't wake up. He died this afternoon."

We found it hard to believe, because we had kissed him goodbye before we left for the party. What did it mean? What was going to happen? We were full of questions:

"Won't we ever see him again?"

12.1 Diana and Mary at Hoover's children's party

"When will he go to heaven?"

"Will he be buried?" we asked.

"Yes, but children won't be allowed at the funeral, and so Aunty Phyl and Uncle Reg are going to look after you until the funeral is over."

We could tell Mum was upset and then we all started crying. Mum knew this would happen and thought having Nipper with us would be a comfort, and although he was frightened to be in the car, he snuggled against my shoulder for the rest of the journey.

It seemed like the middle of the night when we arrived at Wood Green and were greeted by our relations who were keen to make us feel welcome. Before long we were given a bedtime drink in our cousins' special Horlicks mugs, and we slept in Michael's bedroom at the front of the house because Michael (then 19) was away doing his National Service.

The next morning Aunty Phyl woke us up in time to watch from the bedroom window as Mum and Dad drove away with Nipper glaring from the rear window of the car. Aunty Phyl put her arms round us and said:

"Let's dry those tears; you'll be able to talk to Mum and Dad this evening when they ring to see how you are getting on. They'll want to talk to you and hear what you've been doing today, and that you're happy here with us at Wood Green."

True enough for the next couple of weeks Mum or Dad walked down Primrose Hill every evening to speak to us on Mr. White's telephone and make sure we were alright. We looked forward to their phone calls, but just to hear Mum and Dad's voices reduced us to tears again, as we tried to come to terms with the loss of Grampy and what had happened to our family.

Mary and I settled in at 79 Wolves Lane, Wood Green. Our Aunt and Uncle's house was large in comparison with Finchers, and they had an upstairs – a novelty to bungalow-dwellers. Uncle Reg had a genial manner and always made us laugh, Aunty Phyl was kindly and competent with a reassuring manner, and Renee (then 14) held a special place in our affection because, to us, she was good fun and brought new games on her regular visits in the school holidays.

Mary and I spent most of the day with Aunty Phyl; she took us to the pictures one afternoon and, when out shopping, she suggested we spend our pocket money on a red tin tray decorated with two black and white Scottish terriers, as a gift for Mum.

Renee provided us with our own exercise books and helped us with reading and writing. We wrote about the novelty of watching *Children's Hour* on their television set. Our relations at Wood Green were the only people we knew who had a television: they said they were lucky to live near the Alexandra Palace* television studios and

_____

* *In 1951 there were only two television transmitters in Britain – London and Birmingham. Television sets were expensive (up to 76 guineas or three months' average wage) and only 9% of homes owned one.*

transmitter which gave good reception. Mary and I were glued to the television for programmes like *Prudence Kitten* and *Muffin the Mule* accompanied by Annette Mills on the piano. Children's programmes were introduced by a delightful teenage continuity announcer called Jennifer Gay; she was an inspiration.

When Mum and Dad collected us for our return to Finchers, we found things had changed. We each had a bed in Grampy's newly decorated bedroom, and Mum had cut Grampy's large white counterpane in half and dyed it blue, making a cover for each bed. Thrilled with this new arrangement, we were soon in trouble for laughing and shrieking as we jumped and bounced higher and higher on our own beds. Mum was undoubtedly disturbed to hear our laughter and apparent disrespect coming from what had always been Grampy's room; when pushed she would rattle her kitchen utensils and threaten to take out her wooden spoon, but the threat was sufficient, we complied and the wooden spoon never appeared.

Grampy had gone, there was a gap in our family, his empty Windsor chair remained by the fire, and we sometimes sat in it. I don't recall a great deal being said about our loss but we knew Mum and Dad were sad. As usual, we were encouraged to carry on as best we could and try to find positive aspects to the tremendous change in our lives.

13

Christmas Past

Shopping trips with Mum to High Wycombe were planned around the bus service which terminated at the foot of Primrose Hill. It ran only four times a day, every three hours from nine o'clock. Failure to catch this service meant an extra 10-minute walk to and from the next stop (at Cosy Corner) where the buses ran every 30 minutes.

The London Transport Bus Depot in High Wycombe was at the bottom of Marlow Hill just round the corner from Queen Victoria Road. In the 1950s Queen Victoria Road was the municipal centre of High Wycombe; on the west side was the town hall and library and on the east, the municipal offices and post office; these last three buildings were built during the 1930s and looked very solid and imposing.

Next to the post office (and on the crossroads where Queen Victoria Road went straight over to Crendon Street, and where the High Street went east into Easton Street) was Davy's, a stationer and a marvellous toyshop.

Our trips to High Wycombe always ended with time in the library because outside was the stop for our return journey to Primrose Hill. When there was time, we would cross the road to look in the toy shop windows. They were crammed full of all the toys we could ever imagine – soft toys of all sorts: teddy bears, pandas; china dolls, some with eyes that opened and closed, others with silky blonde hair; doll's prams on springs or collapsible; doll's houses of various designs and sizes; bicycles and scooters; tennis and footballs, racquets and bats;

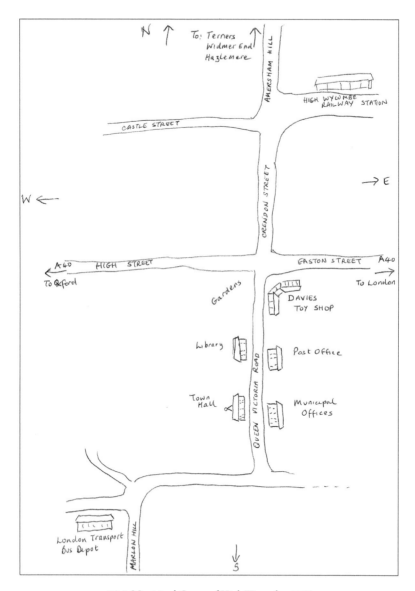

13.1 Municipal Centre of High Wycombe, 1950

games like jacks, marbles, five stones; red, blue and green kites, both diamond and box shaped; and board games like Ludo, Tiddlywinks and snakes and ladders. Mary and I would stand gazing in the window deciding what we liked best. Mary always knew what she wanted for her birthday and Christmas but I found it difficult to decide.

"After I've had *Heidi* for my birthday, I think I'd like a doll's house for Christmas," said Mary and liking the idea, I suggested:

"We could play with the dolls in their house and put them to bed upstairs." Upstairs being a novelty to us bungalow-dwellers.

All the while Mum would be looking out for our bus coming round the corner, and we would hurry across at the traffic lights to catch it.

Stir-up Sunday at the end of November indicated Christmas was coming. Mum had increased our grocery order with things like brown sugar, dried raisins, sultanas and currants, nuts and spices. One evening she would put the shrivelled dried fruit in a basin to soak and the next day they would be plump and ready for mixing. In her large bowl on the kitchen table, she started adding all the ingredients to make three Christmas puddings. Mary and I would be watching intently, hoping to lick the spoon:

"Why are you pouring some of Dad's rum in?" Mary asked.

"That's to make sure the puddings last and don't go off. One of them has to keep 'til Easter Day." Then we saw some Guinness being added:

"And the bottle of black beer? Does that make the puddings last?" and Mum replied:

"No, the stout gives the puddings body and strength. Now it's your turn to stir the pudding and make a wish." Mary went first:

"I shall wish for…"

"No! You mustn't tell anyone what you wish for or it won't come true."

And so, we all took it in turns to stir and make a wish. A handful of silver three-penny pieces were thrown in – these were saved from year to year and reused because they were no longer legal tender, but relics from our mother's childhood in London. The puddings were poured into basins, covered with greaseproof paper, pudding cloths tied on with string and then boiled for 5 or 6 hours. The boiling time was reduced after Mum became the proud owner of a pressure cooker; Mum enjoyed using it, but we found the hissing sounds most alarming. The preparation of the Christmas cake followed soon after, but this time she made only one.

The build-up of excitement for Christmas involved journeys in the car, starting with a Saturday afternoon shopping at Slough where the shops were crowded with people and bright lights. Sometimes we were taken to London, to see the lights, or a visit to Father Christmas at Selfridges, riding in a swan along a waterway to the fairy grotto.

Knowing it pleased Mum to have a meal there, Dad would endure the wait for a table at Lyons Corner House, Marble Arch. In the downstairs dining room, the waitresses, in smart black dresses with white aprons and frilled hats, served us at the table and Mum and Dad smiled at each other as they listened to the Palm Court Trio playing their favourite Ivor Novello tunes from shows like *The Dancing Years*.

Next came visits to our Farmbrough cousins at Wood Green and our mother's uncle and aunt at Enfield. On the return journey we looked out for Christmas lights on some of the factories as we drove round the North Circular Road and along the Western Avenue. At our turn to Beaconsfield, we anticipated the dark country road where Enid Blyton lived at Green Hedges. Some of the large houses had outdoor Christmas lights that shone out in the gloom:

"This house has a Christmas tree all lit up. What can you see on your side?"

Mary was peering from her side of the car, and I spotted something on mine:

"There's this sleigh and reindeer coming over the rooftop." Mary came over my side and said:

"Isn't that wonderful, how do they do that?"

At school we were preparing for Christmas concerts.

Mary and I often coloured our own Christmas cards for school friends. These were posted in a box outside Mr. Dowell the headmaster's office and delivered on the last afternoon before the school broke up. Then there were Christmas parties to attend, organised by the Sunday

13.2 Diana in school concert (middle L4)

School and the Young Wives' Group. These parties followed the same pattern: a game of musical chairs followed by sandwiches and jelly seated at a long table, then a game of pass the parcel. Father Christmas appeared with a gift for each child, and balloons for those who wanted them; and a flurry of donning outdoor clothes as parents arrived to take children home.

Dad dug up our Christmas tree from the garden on the last weekend before the big day, and the box of decorations and lights, stored in the roof for the remainder of the year, were brought out. Being very temperamental, it took ages to get the lights working and arranged on the tree, their twinkle reminding us of the magic that was about to happen.

At last Christmas Eve arrived; Dad came home from work early. A tradition had grown from the time Dad became the first of his siblings to own a car: Mary and I thought we were visiting our cousins to wish them a "Happy Christmas", but unknown to us, the parents were exchanging presents in the kitchen while we children played in their front room with our cousins, usually round their Christmas tree.

The route started in Hazlemere, with our Farmbrough cousins at Penn Road, then on to Grove Road for our Kilroy cousins, next stop Bowerdean Road for our cousin Rosemary Bowles, then on to Widmer End for our Barker cousins, ending up at Holmer Green where Aunty Pauline, her husband Reg and our cousin Geoffrey Osborne lived. It would be getting late by this time and Geoffrey would be in bed, but not asleep, and he would show us drawings of aircraft, trains and cars that he had been working on.

Undoubtedly Mum and Dad were hoping all this travelling would tire us out. On the contrary, once home, we went straight to the fireplace in the front room and made sure Dad's sea-boot socks and our pillowcases, along with a glass of sherry and a mince pie, were set out ready for the great man. Eventually exhaustion set in and we fell asleep wondering what surprises the morning would bring.

1951 was the first Christmas Mary and I had a bedroom of our own. Between our beds was a bedside cabinet with a table lamp and at the foot of Mary's bed was a small wardrobe, on top of which were our two painted alabaster penguins, souvenirs from our daytrip to Chessington Zoo.

Mary and I had a reputation for waking up early on Christmas morning and this first Christmas in our own room was no exception. When we opened our eyes there was a glow coming from the bottom of our beds and a pattern of light on the ceiling. As we sat up and climbed closer, there were lights coming from the windows of the loveliest, shoulder-height doll's house.

It was a traditional, two-storey, mock-Tudor design with two windows on each side, and a further window with a balcony, forming a porch over the central door. Peering through the windows we could see curtains, carpets, wallpaper, furniture, and a family of four small dolls sitting at the kitchen table, waiting for us to start their imagined life.

"Look what Father Christmas has brought us: a doll's house with lights."

"I wonder how you open it to get inside?"

Mum and Dad had heard us whispering:

"Aren't you two lucky that Father Christmas managed to bring you such a lovely present? But come along now, don't you know it's only five o'clock, you will have to get back into bed until its daytime." Dad was firm but kind.

"Alright, but can we keep the doll's house lights on?"

As we settled back in bed:

"What names shall we give the dolls?"

Nothing could compare with the hours of fun we envisaged as we moved our dolls around their house and brought their world to life.

On Christmas morning we always went to church, but Mum sometimes stayed behind to prepare the Christmas dinner. After the service, Grampy Farmbrough, fresh from singing in the church choir, would join us in the car and we would stop off at The Coppice to pick up Uncle David and his dog Scamp. In the front room the fire would have been lit early, ready for the Christmas dinner to be served on the dining table. As the grown-ups sipped a glass of sherry, a yule log would be wedged on the fire, where it would burn for the rest of the day.

"Let's have a toast to a Merry Christmas and a Happy New Year."

"Ditto Repeato" was Uncle David's unfailing response.

We usually had a capon, carved by Dad as head of the household, accompanied with stuffing, vegetables from our garden and gravy. Afterwards the Christmas pudding was served with cream and rum butter – Mary and I hoping to find a silver three-penny piece, signifying good luck.

While the clearing up was going on in the kitchen, Uncle David, Mary and I would select a jigsaw from our newly arrived presents. Mary, being keen to start setting it out on the table, said,

"We must get all the outside pieces first."

"I'll try to find all the sky pieces," I suggested.

"Ooo-aarh, I'm goin' t'sort out this bridge an' stream," said Uncle David in his broad Bucks accent.

Our parent's bribe to ensure co-operation throughout Christmas was the promise of "Tree Presents". We could see them wrapped and waiting under the Christmas tree. Over a cup of tea and a piece of Christmas cake, these remaining gifts were distributed amongst us all. Socks for Grampy Farmbrough and a scarf for Uncle David, a book, gloves, or a packet of hankies – all unwrapped in turn and commented on. As the day drew to a close, Dad would run Grampy Farmbrough back to The Coppice along with the third Christmas pudding. Uncle David and Scamp would set off to walk home through The Park.

On Boxing Day there was very little time to play with our doll's house, because in the afternoon, we changed into our best dresses for a Christmas party. Our hosts were Aunty Pauline and Uncle Reg; Mr and Mrs Osborne senior, Uncle Reg's sister Peg and her family, the Bowles family and sometimes the Barker family would also be there.

The party started with everyone standing, talking, and moving around the ground floor; the first game had already started: we were looking for items clearly out of place (a thimble perched on a picture frame, or a rubber band round an apple). After a buffet tea eaten on our laps, using pencil and paper we made a list of the items spotted. Roars of laughter erupted as Uncle Reg went round and collected them up – we had all missed so many! It became even more hilarious as we played Kim's Game and Passing the Scissors. Then, when the sherry, dates and nuts came out, so did the cards. Simple games like Rummy and Newmarket, played for pennies and fiercely fought over, lasted well past our bedtime.

In those days only the schools closed for longer than two days at Christmas. After Boxing Day, it was back to work as usual. For working people, the next holiday would be Easter.

14

Our Dad – The Joy of the Open Road – Cornwall

It must have been in the spring of 1938 that Grampy Farmbrough, then still an active fifty-nine-year-old, said to his youngest son Pete:

"I think it's time for us to go down to Cornwall on my motorbike and visit Mrs Pope at Lelant."

"Gosh, that would be great, imagine what the blokes at work will say when I tell them I'm going to Cornwall on holiday." Pete was an inquisitive eighteen-year-old and very keen for any sort of adventure.

Two years earlier, Pete's eldest brother, Jack, had married Eileen Pope and their first child, Dennis, had arrived and twins were due in the autumn. Grampy Farmbrough undoubtedly saw merit in maintaining close ties with the mother of his daughter-in-law, Mrs Pope. So, he took up the casual invitation to:

"Visit us in Cornwall at any time. We can always put you up."

They travelled light, on an underpowered motorbike. They joined the A30 at Basingstoke and followed it to Cornwall. Pete enjoyed the experience; it was the first time he had been so far from home, and he was captivated by the ever-changing scenery as they drove over Cranborne Chase in Hampshire, and through Winchester and Exeter, towns he had only ever heard about. But he was frustrated at his father's sedate progress at 30 miles an hour. Six hours after setting out they reached the edge of Dartmoor and stayed overnight at Moorlands Hotel, continuing the next morning to Lelant, their destination.

Because Mrs Pope was the local midwife, and could be on call, it was arranged for them to stay with Mrs Old, a cheery middle-aged widow:

"Come on in m'dears, make yourselves at home." She led the way upstairs.

"I've got this nice room for you with good views over the Towans* to the sea. When you've settled in, come down and take a cup of tea wi' me."

Later she took them a few houses down the road to meet Mrs. Pope and filled them in on the way:

"I'm very happy to help out with B&B for you m'dears; Mrs Pope's very highly regarded locally; you might almost say she's an institution."

Once the formalities with Mrs Pope were dispensed with, Pete was free to escape, savour the tang of salt in the air and to roam the wild and beautiful area within a short walk of Lelant. The wide vistas over the Towans and out to sea, and the small, stonewalled fields were in total contrast to the Chiltern Hills he had grown up with, and it seemed to him wildflowers were growing at every turn. For Pete it was an unforgettable experience and one he frequently referred to in later life.

Twelve years later, Pete had become the proud owner of a 1935 Hillman Minx and, as his confidence with the vehicle grew, he wanted to introduce Sybil, Mary now coming up to five, and me six, to the excitement, wonder and joy he had experienced on his 1938 holiday, and so, as soon as petrol came off the ration in May 1950, he said to Sybil:

"We should think about going to stay with Mrs. Old in Lelant. I'm sure the old car will get us down to Cornwall alright."

"That sounds wonderful, what an adventure. I'd love to go, but we must take care that the strain of all that driving won't be too much

---

*   *Towans is the Cornish name for sand dunes; these were on the Hayle Estuary between the fields and the sea at St. Ives Bay. Undoubtedly Pete and Sybil, then married for eight years, appreciated the romance of wandering over the dunes at sunset.*

for you." Sybil knew that Pete's bronchiectasis could be a problem at unexpected times.

"Won't it be lovely to see the girls enjoying the fresh air and playing on the beach?"

"We shall have to keep a close check on our spending, so we can afford the petrol." Sybil was practical as ever.

Preparations were made for the trip: Grampy Rackstraw's friend Mr Hanks would come to stay, and Eva Saunders, our next-door neighbour, would take in a hot meal and keep an eye on them. Our holiday essentials, change of underwear, nightwear, flannel and toothbrush each were packed in one small suitcase which was placed on the rear luggage rack, covered with a groundsheet to keep the rain off and tied down with a strong rope. Our buckets and spades were stowed behind the back seat inside the car, along with the primus stove and tea-making gear. We all travelled in our best clothes.

Sybil kept a journal:

Filled up with petrol before leaving.	6 gallons		18s	6d
28/7/50				
Started at 1.30pm				
Tea outside Salisbury 5pm				
Stayed night Moorlands Hotel, Cheriton Cross, very comfortable.				
Bed and Breakfast		£2	7s	0d
Petrol	3 gallons		9s	6d

Travelling in the Hillman Minx was comfortable; it had deep maroon leather seats and there were strap hangers with thick tassels for the passengers to hold when cornering. There were cord mesh pockets on the doors and the dashboard was walnut veneer.

Mary and I chose to stand up for most of the journey. When

behind Dad, Mary would reach over his shoulder and take his comb from the top pocket of his sports jacket. Dad allowed her to comb the back of his hair as the miles clocked up. Sometimes we fluttered our handkerchiefs outside our windows.

29/7/50			
Phoned Mrs White from Whiddon Down PO 8.30	Phone call	3s	11d
Stopped Jamaica Inn for coffee 10.45			
Lelant 1.00			
St Ives, Carbis Bay in afternoon			
Walked on Towans in evening	3 gallons	9s	6d
	Post cards	1s	6d
	Stamps	2s	0d

The phone call was to our neighbour Mrs White, asking her to pass on a vital message for Grampy Rackstraw, left at home. The significance of the stop at Jamaica Inn would have been appreciated by Sybil, a keen reader of Daphne du Maurier. The drive that morning over the rugged and dramatic scenery of Dartmoor and Bodmin Moor undoubtedly increased the excitement as we travelled deeper into Cornwall. After leaving the A30 at Hayle, Mary and I spotted a brightly coloured advertising hoarding, with flowers round the edge, saying:

"SEND MUM AND DAD AND AUNTY GLAD
ANEMONIES AND VIOLETS BY POST"

This amused us and, during our stay, we looked out for and recited the verse each time we passed, and many more times in the years ahead.

14.1 Lelant, Mrs Old's cottage at far end of terrace

By early afternoon Mrs. Old had welcomed us to Lelant and settled us in our rooms.

Lelant is on the north coast of Cornwall, only 12 miles from Land's End, on the road to Carbis Bay and St. Ives. How thrilled Sybil must have been as the places she had only ever heard of became a reality.

30/7/50			
Rain in morning, went up Trencrom, ride round and into St. Ives.			
Land's End in afternoon. Misty unable to see anything.			
Followed coastline to Penzance, Mousehole and Newlyn. Dangerous			
Road to Lamorna Cove, very unsuitable but lived to tell the tale.			

Tea at Land's End. Visibility about 20 yds. Back through Penzance 7.30			
Bed at 1 o'clock after good gossip.			
	3 gallons	9s	3d
	Postcards	3s	0d

About a mile inland from Lelant is an ancient hill fort called Trencrom, 500ft above sea level, with huge rocky outcrops. Pete had climbed Trencrom on his first visit and knew Sybil and we girls would love the sensation from the top. So, as soon as the rain stopped, we set off.

"Well, fancy having a view to the sea on both sides, I can even pick out St. Michael's Mount," said Sybil. Pete was glad this place had made a favourable impression, and replied:

"I read this is one of the few places in Britain where the sun rises and sets over the sea."

Mary and I had been running around the top of the hill, and called out:

"Look at us, climbing over these giant stones."

Sybil frowned:

"Just be careful, we don't want any accidents on these rocks."

That evening, after Mary and I were in bed, Mrs Old came into our room and drawing back the curtain said:

"Now its dark m'dears, let me show you the Godrevy Lighthouse."

We peered through the window into the darkness, and then saw a flash of light:

"Why does it flash and not stay on all the time?" we asked and Mrs Old explained:

"Each lighthouse has its own pattern of light, so the sailors can tell which lighthouse it is, and keep away from those dangerous rocks."

So, then we wondered:

14.2 Mum with Diana and Mary at Trencrom

"Are there any ships out there in the dark tonight?"

Mrs. Old looked very thoughtful and told us there had been many tragedies on Godrevy Point but then sought to put our minds at rest by saying:

"When there's a wreck, all the folk hereabouts go down to the coast to help save the poor sailors and get them safely ashore."

31/7/50

Walked on beach at Lelant all morning very nice and quiet.

Took Mrs Old to Land's End in afternoon, saw Scilly Isles 40 miles away also Wolf Rock Lighthouse. Had tea in a field, went to Marazion. Good view of St Michaels Mount. Came back via Sennen Cove, St Just and Zennor.

The next morning, as we followed a footpath to the sea across the field beside Mrs Old's cottage, we came across a ruined tin mine. Pete told us what it was and he said:

"Some of these tin mines are really old, the Romans came to Cornwall for the tin. It was an important trade and the Cornish have mined tin for generations." Mary and I were curious,

"Why is this mine a ruin?"

Pete explained:

"When the ore runs out, they try elsewhere. Tin miners had ancient rights to open up a mine and this made them very independent spirited."

Sybil joined in at this point:

"Mrs Old said that Cornish pasties contain a complete meal for the tin miners to take underground with them – but would you want to eat down there in the dark?" We turned up our noses and didn't fancy it.

The "Danger Keep Out" sign did not deter Pete from tossing a stone down the dark hole to see how deep it was. Hearing an immediate "chink" was a disappointment.

14.3 Beach at Lelant, Diana and Mary in distance

1/8/1950

Started at 10am for Newquay. Nice clean town. Left at 1pm for Tintagel via Wadebridge arrived 3.10 left 4.30.

Magnificent rocks and granite formations and ruins of King Arthur's Castle. Made for Bude via Boscastle. Fish & Chips at Bude. Clovelly at 7.30pm Very quaint and cobblestoned High Street almost perpendicular. Made for Bideford next arrived at Lagoon camping site at 9.30pm Slept in car. Terrific storm during night. Kept dry alright. Left 9.30am.

Petrol and Garage		16s	0d
Mrs Old	£7	10s	0d
Fish & Chips		3s	0d
Camp Site		2s	6d

14.4 Mary, Sybil, and Diana at Clovelly

2/8/50

Made for Ilfracombe. Torrential downpour of rain lasted about 3 hours. Left Ilfracombe 2pm Very good dinner Roast Chicken. Made for Lynton. Lovely wooded scenery. Very dangerous bends and hilly about 1 in 3 in places. Scenery at Watersmeet was marvellous. Had to have two goes to get round a bend. Descended in low gear to East Lynn up another hill for about 5 miles, Exmoor at top, still very hilly. Lovely scenery. Porlock Hill was terribly steep, but lovely view over Porlock from the top. Stopped for tea just outside Minehead. Made for Glastonbury in evening. Very quaint town (old fashioned). Stopped at Polsham Station for Bed and Breakfast. Quite good.

Petrol	10s	11d
Dinner	17s	0d
Coffee	2s	0d
Postcards	1s	4d
Stamps	2s	0d
Postcards	2s	0d

3 August 1950 (Sybil's birthday)

Wookey Hole Caves at 9.15am. Very wet inside, but extremely interesting. Rock formations weird especially the witch and her dog, also a turkey in the rock. Cheddar caves next, there the rock formations are coloured including the stalactites and stalagmites. Liked Wookey best. Wells next, had dinner - indifferent. Looked over the cathedral, very impressive and in excellent state of repair. Went to a short service. Saw the clock strike and the soldier go round. Started for Bath 3.30. Then home.

Bed and Breakfast	£1	10s	0d
Petrol and oil		10s	1d
Wookey Caves		5s	0d
Cheddar Caves		5s	0d
Dinner		11s	0d

Total cost of trip, 26 July–3 August 1950 (7 nights)   £18 2s 4d

*(2022 equivalent – £665)**

What is the true value of a holiday? Is it purely for rest and recreation, or should a holiday bring new experiences and a fresh outlook on life? Is a change as good as a rest? For our little family, the evidence points to all of these.

The year that followed this holiday brought death, illness, and heartache. In February 1951 Grampy Rackstraw, our beloved "Grampy", died of pneumonia. With his death, Pete was forced to evaluate the reality of his and Sybil's dream of building their own home and running a small holding. Three factors were against them: firstly without Grampy's help and support, Pete's unreliable health meant he would struggle to manage the land on his own; secondly building societies would not lend money to people who already had a home of their own; and thirdly the government introduced a tax on unbuilt land with planning permission, eroding any benefit from the undeveloped land. Their dream faded and, reluctantly, they sold the land.

In the spring of that year, Mary and I, both now at school, caught measles and Sybil nursed us while we were isolated at home.

It is hardly surprising that Pete and Sybil wanted to put these troubles behind them and repeat the joyous experience of the holiday in Cornwall. And so the following year, we stayed with Mrs. Curnow, a friend of Mrs Old, who lived at Carbis Bay.

On this holiday in 1951, many places were re-visited, more time was spent on the beach at Carbis Bay and a permanent souvenir

---

*   *(The conversion of £1 in 1950 equates to £36.51 in 2022 – source: CPI inflation calculator).*

14.5 Outside Mrs. Curnow's house, Carbis Bay

barometer from the Lizard, made of green Serpentine rock, was brought back. This barometer was kept on an outside wall of the front room at Finchers, and later at Pete and Sybil's other homes. After their demise, now (seventy years later) it has pride of place in Hilary's hallway at Mill House in Bridgham and is still reliable.

14.6 Mary and Diana at a gift shop at the Lizard (barometers on wall)

15

Schooldays

Our School, Hazlemere Church of England

Down a narrow path is the Victorian schoolhouse where the headmistress lives, with three infant classrooms behind.

September 1949. I hold hands with my cousin Geoffrey. Nervously we watch our mums walk away. He cries, I squeeze his hand and hold back my tears.

We join the infant's school at age five for two years. Strange smells of plasticine, sand in trays and wax crayons; windows so high we can only see clouds; how different from home.

Outside lavatories, smelly and dark.

Geoffrey leaves our school when his family move to Holmer Green, and I miss him.

Soon I am on the Robins' table with the best readers.

15.2 Geoffrey Osborne

85

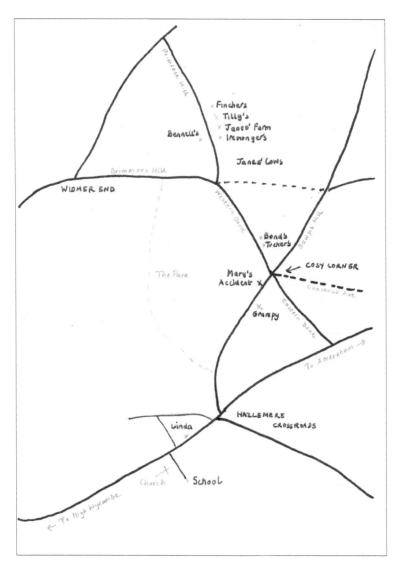

15.1 The route to school

In the big school for the next four years. Junior 1, the whole class learns to knit a dishcloth – it takes a year.

Junior 2, we learn cursive writing and copy "Monday, 10th September 1952" from the blackboard.

Monday mornings. Assembly in the school hall, ink pots filled, register checked, dinner money paid. I buy a "Squirrel" National Savings Stamp; this money is to fund my uniform when I pass the 11+ exam.

At playtime boys climb trees and race over heaps of soil at the bottom of the field. Girls play 'Oranges and Lemons', clapping games, two balls and skipping. They join the boys for conkers, chasing and sliding on the ice.

Oranges and lemons:
Oranges and lemons say the bells of St. Clements,
You owe me five farthings say the bells of St. Martins,
When will you pay me say the bells of Old Bailey?
When I grow rich say the bells of Shoreditch.
When will that be say the bells of Stepney?
I do not know says the great bell of Bow.

A skipping rhyme:
The wind, the wind, the wind blows high,
The rain comes scattering from the sky,
She is handsome she is pretty; she is the girl from the golden city,
She has a sweetheart, one two three,
Please tell me who is he?

Junior 3. Miss Shippey enforces discipline with a wooden ruler or the slipper (plimsoll). The class watches as the culprit receives a stroke on the hand or bottom; or if serious, is sent to stand under the clock outside the headmaster's office. We learn a poem a week:

Home Thoughts, from Abroad by Robert Browning
Loveliest of Trees, the Cherry Now by AE Housman
Little Trotty Wagtail by John Clare
Sir Nicketty Nox by Hugh Chesterman
The Snare I hear a sudden cry of pain by James Stephens

Tuesday mornings. Whole school assembly followed by "Singing". We learn well-known hymns and songs from the National Song Book.

Jerusalem: *a wonderful tune with words about building a new Jerusalem in England's green and pleasant land.*
All Things Bright and Beautiful: *which confirmed our place in the natural world around us, all part of God's gift.*
Immortal, Invisible, God Only Wise: *about the mystery of God being in a pavilion.*
Will Ye No Come Back Again? *A sad Scottish song about Bonnie Prince Charlie's escape to France.*
Men of Harlech: *a jolly Welsh march always sung loudly.*

Dinner time in the canteen. A regimented, disheartening experience; steamed-up canteen, tasteless food; enlivened by Kristina Kant, one of the children from The Polish Resettlement Camp*, who teaches us *Dzien dobry* (good day) and *Chodz tu* (come here).

Ash Wednesday. Whole school service in freezing cold church: we are encouraged to search our souls in preparation for forty days of abstinence during Lent. Always a problem; we wonder what to give up.

---

* *Hazlemere Park, a former manor house and grounds, was taken over by the military in 1940 and the Royal Engineers moved in and remained for the duration of the war. At the end of the war as the troops left, soldiers of the Polish Carpathian Brigade moved in awaiting demobilisation, and gradually, fifty families occupied the army huts, and it became known as The Hazlemere Polish Resettlement Camp. The camp was well organised; there was a Polish church with their own priest and Christmas parties. The children who attended Hazlemere School were learning English for the first time. The camp was closed during the 1950s as the families were rehoused.*

Summer term. Sports day on the field, sack race, three-legged race, running, good fun but no prizes for me. On another sunny afternoon, there is a formal prize giving on the Vicarage lawn, when important people we don't recognise hand out books, and most children receive a prize.

Junior 4. Spring 1955, the 11+ exam means relentless preparations, homework, mental arithmetic, spelling, and Intelligence tests. Our form teacher Mr. Edgerley's diligence is rewarded, all those who cleared the preliminary exam have passed, however only eight places are allocated to our school, four boys and four girls.

I am not one of them.

At the end of the school day, we lift our chairs on our desks, put our hands together and pray for God to lighten our darkness and defend us from the perils and dangers of the night, before grabbing our coats and running up the school path to catch the bus home.

15.4 Diana at school

My Best Friend

In 1951 a dainty girl with wiry mouse-coloured hair sits next to me in class. Her name is Margaret Reed, at home she is called Margot.

We make friends straightaway; we are both seven and spend our break and dinner times together. We discover a shared interest in reading, and nature.

Margot and I can name everything on the nature table; she brings items from their nine-acre orchard, and I have no trouble finding cowslips, primroses, or something seasonal from the abundant roadside verges and hedgerows on the way to the bus stop; Margot's mother drives her to school.

Margot and I are both collecting Flower Fairies books by Cicely Mary Barker; we love the illustrations which fuel our imaginations and help weave a magical world of dreams and reality.

Margot comes to tea with us at Finchers and then I am invited to Freshwinds, her house for the day. I make friends with their King Charles Cocker Spaniel, Gaylord de Fontenay, or Gay.

Behind their house is a tennis court, and we get out some racquets and pretend to play, then we wander into their apple orchard and find a disused swimming pool.

"Do you ever put water in it?" I ask Margot.

"There's no one to keep the water clean, it's always full of leaves."

Margot's father is a wholesale fruiterer in Aylesbury; he drives the latest pale green Sunbeam Alpine car, and Margot's mother drives his old car. Mrs. Reed has shoulder-length dark hair simply arranged with a tortoiseshell hairband – she wears neat, tailored slacks and a bright coloured twinset, smokes cigarettes, and has red lipstick and red nails; her voice is lilting and kind.

A bell sounds and we go back to the house for mid-morning drinks in the cosy kitchen with Mrs. Reed and her "daily". Later, in the conservatory, Margot says:

"Shall we have a go with this Plaster of Paris Set I had for my birthday?"

Fascinated I ask:

"How does it work; what do you have to do?"

We mix the powdery plaster of Paris with water and fill red rubber moulds in the shape of different animals. I could see model spaniels already drying in a rack, and said:

"Aren't these models lovely, they are just like Gay."

We paint a completed model spaniel with the same markings as Gay.

Margot has an older sister, Paula, and a brother, John, who is at university.

When her brother comes home, the family eat in the formal dining room. Confronted with everyone talking and laughing, it's much noisier than mealtimes at Finchers, and I am self-conscious. I can hardly speak or eat a thing. Margot smiles at me to show she understands, and afterwards she says:

"Don't take any notice of John, he's always showing off."

15.6 School concert – Margot top left, Diana bottom right 7

For three years our friendship softens the formalities and rituals of the school year. On the day of the 11+ exam results, both our form teacher, Mr. Edgerly and the headmaster, Mr Dowell, come into the classroom together. Mr. Dowell is holding a piece of paper in his hand; in a stern voice he tells us that all those who passed the preliminary examination have done well, but our school is allocated only eight places: four boys will go to the Royal Grammar School and four girls to Wycombe High School. He then reads out the names.

Margot goes on to the High School and I stay at Hazlemere.

Letter to My Schoolgirl Self

My dear little Diana,

You have made a good start, you like your first school uniform, your leather satchel and the double wooden pencil case that swivels and has a sliding top.

You fit in well with the other children and you are doing what is expected, you make the best of where you are. Without exception you will find the teachers at Hazlemere School distant and cold; you in return, will afford them respect and co-operation. These are the skills you need to navigate life.

There are two important things I must tell you about the 11+ exam.

The first is about Mum and Dad's attitude and determination for you to pass. They don't intend to put pressure on you, it is their own way of dealing with the Buckinghamshire Education Committee. Mum and Dad had both separately been told when at your age, "You will not be sitting the 11+ exam, because your parent(s) can't afford the school uniform even if you pass", and so they want to prove, through you, that they *did* have the ability to succeed in the exam.

The second thing is about the year of your birth. You were born at the end of the Second World War when servicemen and women were returning home and starting (or adding to) families. There was a population explosion. At first you were part of "the bulge year," but the bulge went on until 1956 and the Bucks Education Committee was overwhelmed and hastily adjusting. That is why in Mr. Edgerley's class, Mum and Dad bought extra revision books for English, Arithmetic, and Intelligence, they wanted to give you the best advantage.

Mum and Dad's disappointment was mollified by the fact that your cousins Molly and Rosemary didn't get places either. There were more important things to think about that year: your family were about to move to a new house and was looking forward to the arrival of your sister (Hilary) who was born in August.

The solution to the demographic bulge was found, and by 1957, successful 13+ students were given places at The Technical College - now redesignated for boys only and the girls were awarded places at the newly created Lady Verney High School in the former Wycombe High School premises. You and your cousins (belatedly) gained a higher education.

You belong to a generation of children who are generally well behaved, keen to learn, good natured and optimistic. What you learn at school is as important as *how* to learn. You will apply this knowledge again and again to progress your career and ensure you are never out of work. Your life will not be easy, you will struggle against restrictive social attitudes and injustices towards women, there will be heartache and grief in the home and in the workplace. You will eventually overcome, and when you look back you will be amazed at how things have changed.

Have courage, your future awaits,
from your older, happier and contented self
in the year 2022.

Walking to School

During the first ten years of my life, when we lived at Primrose Hill deep in the Chilterns, most of the walking we did was to and from school.

I started school a year ahead of my sister Mary; once she joined me, each morning Mum would comb our hair as we recited our times tables, a poem or whatever we had been learning, then she would send us off with our bus money and satchels on our backs.

We turned left and called for our schoolmates down the hill.

Alan Tilly lived next door but one to us and his mum would be waiting at their back door, she was friendly and generous. On non-school days when we played with Alan, she could be relied on for homemade Rice Krispy cakes. Alan emerged, he was always smartly dressed: you felt his mum had polished him, whether for school or play; he was younger than me, short and stocky with dark hair and, being an only child, always eager to walk with us.

Further down the hill we knocked on the back door of the three Bennell children, who lived in the last house on the right-hand side.

The Bennells' back garden sloped down into the valley between Primrose Hill and Widmer End. They had enough land to keep pigs as well as chickens and rabbits. I remember Mrs. Bennell taking us to the bottom of their land to show us wild bee orchids. She was a real country-loving woman. One spring she took all the Primrose Hill children on a ramble to the far side of Spurlands End and down a footpath into a bluebell wood. She called out "Hello" and to our surprise back came an echo: *"Hello"*. Of course, we all started calling at once and it didn't work, so she made us take turns. Then we picked armfulls of bluebells to take home.

Susan Bennell was a year older than me and had dark curly hair; Jimmy and John both younger, had auburn hair. Waiting at their back door, we heard their mum in a fluster, calling to us:

"This power cut 'as put us all behind."

Then to her children:

"Johnny, where's yer shoes? Susan, get yer coat on and help Jimmy wiv 'is buttons."

Power cuts were common, but our Mum used the Courtier Stove to cook our porridge and boil a kettle.

Our party of six chattering children descended the steepest part of Primrose Hill. We walked on the road, there were no pavements. In the spring we saw the hawthorn hedges turning green, and on the verges, recognised wildflowers from our Flower Fairies books; dog violets, lords and ladies, colt's-foot, dandelions, daisies, and cow parsley thrusting through the grass.

At the T junction at the foot of the hill a footpath went steeply to the left. We called it "Double Hedges" – it was a shortcut to Holmer Green. This junction was wide enough for the High Wycombe bus to turn round and wait for the next departure on the route that went through Widmer End, Four Ashes and Terriers. It didn't go to Hazlemere, so we had to turn left and walk to the bus stop at Cosy Corner.

On the right side of Western Dene was The Park, bounded by a high hedge that stretched from the top of Holmer Green Road, along Western Dene and up Brimmers Hill. There were lodge cottages at each end and a third near Cosy Corner. The Park was taken over by the military in 1940, and after the war became a Polish Resettlement Camp.

After rain Western Dene was one big puddle. There were drainage ditches but they weren't effectively maintained. Mum had warned us:

"Don't talk to those old men when they come to dig out the ditches. Some of them are wounded soldiers who are best left alone."

We wondered which was worse, the puddles or the old men. To avoid the puddles, we walked on the verges. The boys looked for birds' nests: sparrows were easiest to spot with untidy strands of straw poking out; blackbird nests were better disguised:

"Come an' 'have a look, this 'ere is a Blackie."

And we put our fingers into the nest, felt the mud lining and marvelled at the blue speckled eggs.

"Best to leave 'em alone or the mother bird'll desert."

Our progress had slowed to a dawdle but would quicken when we were joined by Peter Bond and Susan Tucker who lived further along on the sunny bank of Western Dene.

At the bus stop we congregated in separate groups, depending on where we came from: Sawpit Hill, Chestnut Avenue, Eastern Dene and the Polish children from The Park. The small shop behind the bus stop was not one our mother used so we never went inside but looked on enviously as other children emerged with a gobstopper or chewing gum. Eventually, the bus came down Sawpit Hill and we jumped on for the last leg of our journey to school.

One summer Mary and I decided to do something about the "horrible" school dinners. Mary set out our case to Mum and Dad:

"The school dinners are disgusting, the meat is all fat and gristle, and the cabbage smells revolting, it makes me feel sick."

I chimed in:

"Now Mary can ride a two-wheeler, can we ride our bikes to school? We can put them in the school bike shelter, and then we can ride them home for dinner."

Dad had misgivings:

"There's a lot more traffic on Amersham Road these days, I don't think it's safe for you to take your bikes over the crossroads."

Mum intervened with a compromise:

"If you rode your bikes to Grampy's, you could walk the rest of the way to school. There should still be time to eat your dinner here with me and get back to school."

With Grampy's consent, it was agreed. We stopped paying our dinner money and felt very grown-up riding our bikes to The Coppice, our grandfather's house, and leaving them in his garage.

There were pavements all the way from The Coppice to school. At a safe place before reaching the crossroads, we crossed on to the side where there were four shops: Gilbert's Dairy; the Post Office, run by Mr. Manning and his son Norman; Stockton's Butchers; and Claudette's, haberdashers. We followed the path on to Amersham Road, past the Three Horseshoes pub, Ford's Grocers and a few houses set back behind hedges. Mary met her best friend, Linda Oliver, on their first day at school and Linda lived at Corydon towards the end of this row.

"Can you see Linda?"

"No, but there's Grandma Oliver waving out the window, so she's just coming."

(Since those days Linda and Mary's friendship has remained strong throughout their varied and interesting lives.) Outside the headmaster's house was a Belisha beacon crossing. We used it to cross to the top of the school lane, and often met up with the pupils who had just alighted from the bus. We were safely at school at last.

After only a few weeks, the *going home at dinner time* arrangement came to a sudden stop. One lunchtime we had

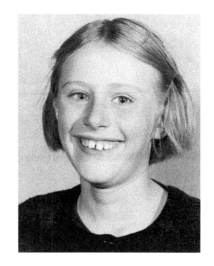

15.7 Mary at school

collected our bikes from Grampy's as usual and were freewheeling down to the bottom of Holmer Green Road, when Mary's front wheel hit a pothole and she was thrown off. I looked at her unconscious body on the road and felt paralysed by fear (was she dead?) and wondered what to do next – when Olive Tucker, Susan's mother, came along on her bike and took control.

"Poor little Mary. We'd better take her back to your grandfather's house." I helped put their bikes into the hedge.

Mary was coming round by this time, and I rode home to get Mum. Back at school that afternoon, I was feeling a bit shocked but very important, knocking on the door and going into Mary's class to say my carefully rehearsed lines:

"Please Miss Alman, Mary can't come to school this afternoon because she's fallen off her bike and got concussion."

At the end of the school day, the bus stop was crowded with children going to Penn as well as Chesham or Ley Hill. If our bus didn't come, one of the boys suggested:

"Let's walk up to the crossroads and if the bus *still* hasn't come, we can put our bus fares together and buy a packet of ice cream wafers from Gilbert's Dairy to eat as we walk down Holmer Green Road."

This seemed very daring, and I was worried:

"What if Mum finds out?"

"Well, just say the bus was late."

We stuck with the group and started to walk.

Ambling home along Western Dene, Peter Bond showed us how to get into The Park. On the other side of the hedge primroses and cowslips grew wild under the bushes.

"We can jump the ditch and squeeze through the hedge here."

"It's a big stride, if I slip, I'll get me shoes muddy."

"Johnny and I will get you girls across."

"Mum would love a bunch of cowslips."

We took a leap and scratched our arms on the thorns, but there they were in the late afternoon sunshine: cowslips glowing brightly and dancing as they poked through the tufts of grass.

We Primrose Hill children would still be together as we turned the corner to climb the hill. We hoped we were ahead of Farmer Janes' cows. The Janes' farm was between Tilly's and the Iremonger's house. His cows processed from the field at the foot of our hill to his farm for milking. Farmer Janes wore an old gaberdine mac tied up with string, he carried a long stick and his dog ran back and forth barking behind the cows. He would shout at us in a high-pitched cackle:

"Ye you'ns k'p awar vrom these 'ere cais."

His Bucks accent was so broad, it was hard to understand. His Friesian cows were lumbering animals; they blocked the road and left big wet cowpats for us to look out for and try to avoid.

Over the years, as we walked to and from school, we watched as the seasons unfolded. The hedges and trees changed colour and lost their leaves. We changed into winter uniform and started wearing gloves and scarves. We collected conkers along Western Dene. The mornings and nights grew darker, we used hand torches because there were no streetlights. Sometimes there was the excitement of frost and snow.

At the end of the school day how glad we were to get back home to Mum in a brightly lit and warm kitchen, our tea of bread and jam on the table and Nipper our cat curled up asleep in front of the stove.

Schooldays (Haiku)

Splashing through puddles
Following older children
Starting out on life's journey.

16

Drama at Cosy Corner

In the summer of 1950, on school days the Primrose Hill children would saunter down the hill and along the bottom to the crossroads at Cosy Corner, where we would wait for the bus. Immediately behind the bus stop was a dilapidated, corrugated iron, general store owned by Billy Dearlove, where children were tempted to use their spare pocket money while waiting.

Billy Dearlove's name cropped up one day when Mum, Dad, Mary and I had made a special visit to see our grandfather at The Coppice. Grampy was on his usual seat in the garden and just round the corner Uncle David was cleaning out his ferrets, so Mary and I went to help him, until something in our grandfather's voice made us listen:

"Who'd a thought it, old Billy Dearlove's been found murdered, in 'is own shop and the takins' has gone missin' as well." Mum and Dad were plainly shocked at this news, but Mum was the first to take it in:

"He was a true cockney, salt of the earth, who'd want to do a thing like that?"

Uncle David left his ferrets and came round the corner to fill in the story:

"The police were down at Cosy Corner soon after they found 'is body. They say 'is 'ands and ankles were tied with 'is own pyjama cord and a sack thrown over 'is 'ead."

Grampy was looking solemn:

"I heard 'e was naked except for 'is vest."

Dad shuffled his feet and looked with concern at us children:

"Well, it's shocking that something like that could 'appen just down the road."

And, thinking about the good nature of the victim, Uncle David added:

"I remember it was Billy Dearlove who first called the crossroads *Cosy Corner*. Mind you, 'e was a 'ard businessman, if there was a penny to be 'ad, 'e would be there."

And Dad, who found it hard to criticise, said:

"Yes, but 'e was well liked, and kind to people in trouble."

It was all quite baffling and we weren't sure whether to be frightened or intrigued, however the following morning we set off for school as usual. We had to wait for the bus at the bottom of Chestnut Avenue, because the area around the shop was cordoned off. Some of the children hadn't heard about the murder, but Peter Bond, was full of it:

"What d'ya think? Billy Dearlove's been murdered. That's why 'is shop is closed up this morning. The police came to see my dad, he says they're looking for the last person to see Billy Dearlove alive."

While still trying to take it all in, someone asked:

"What does a dead person look like? Do you think his shop will be haunted?"

The following week, the school holidays had started, so we were still eating Puffed Wheat for breakfast when Joan our post girl arrived. She was breathless and bubbling with news as usual, her golden curls and bright red lipstick lighting up her face as she stood at the back door, bursting with news:

"The police didn't waste much time. They've identified two suspects, arrested one called Kalinowski – or some such name. The other one, I can't pronounce his name, begins with an "S", well, he's disappeared. Scotland Yard are searching the London Docks."

Mum was intrigued, but anxious:

"I hope they never come anywhere near here again. We don't want murderers in our midst."

"Well, it turns out neither of these Poles are from The Park, so what they were doing at Cosy Corner is a mystery. Anyway, the suspect they've got – he's been working at Slough; and he's going to be tried at the Buckingham Assizes for murder. Well, I must get along. TTFN."

And off she went with her post bag over her shoulder. Mum told us not to worry, the situation was all being dealt with.

Sometime later when we called into The Coppice, Aunty Pauline and Uncle Reg and our cousin Geoffrey were there as well. Grampy Farmbrough was sitting by the fireplace smoking his pipe, we children were by the window talking to Uncle David's wounded linnet in its cage, our parents were standing around the table looking at an open newspaper. We pricked up our ears as Uncle Reg said:

"Can you believe it? That Pole, Kalinowski, has got away with murder, the jury gave him the benefit of the doubt and he's been acquitted – not guilty. It's unbelievable."

Uncle David joined in:

"Yes, 'e said 'e was with Stefanowicz, and they were desperate for money, but 'e always held that 'e waited outside, and never knew Billy Dearlove 'ad been murdered."

Our Dad shook his head:

"I still think that's 'ard to believe."

And Grampy pointed his pipe towards the article in the paper:

"Yes, but he's been re-arrested for burglary, so he's not free – yet."

A few weeks later, Doris, our paper girl, brought the *Bucks Free Press*, and Dad read out, triumphantly:

"They call it the *Cosy Corner Store Burglary*. They've got him at last: that Pole Kalinowski's got 21 months for burglary. It says there were splinters of wood in his turn-ups and green paint found under his fingernails that matched the shop window frame, proving he *was* there and forced the window."

Mum was pleased to hear the news, although she felt strongly:

"But 21 months is no justice for the murder of Billy Dearlove, is it?"

And Dad nodded in agreement.

The story didn't end there. Scotland Yard had traced Stefanowicz to a Russian ship bound for Leningrad via Kiel and Stockholm. The captain wouldn't let Scotland Yard on his ship at Kiel and by the time the ship reached Stockholm, Stefanowicz had already been taken off by a Russian tug.

By September the murder at Cosy Corner turned into an international Cold War incident. We were back at The Coppice, Grampy Farmbrough in his chair as usual; the headline in the open newspaper on the table read *Callous killer in Cosy Corner*, and Uncle David, Mum and Dad were standing round discussing it. Uncle David, running his finger over the article, said:

"Look at this in the paper now: Radio Moscow claims Stefanowicz was a fugitive from British persecution. 'e says 'e was recruited by the British to spy for 'em, and 'e absconded from their school for foreign agents. 'e says the British implicated 'im for murder because 'e refused to spy for 'em."

Jokingly, our Dad said:

"Do y'think this School for Foreign Agents is in The Park?" and everyone chuckled, then Uncle David continued:

"And would you believe it? 'e's been repatriated by the Soviets."

That was when Mum joined in:

"Good riddance to bad rubbish that's what I say. I hope he rots in hell."

There was general agreement, and then Dad spotted the picture:

"And look at the picture in the paper, it's Flint Cottage at Hazlemere Crossroads, it's not Cosy Corner Crossroads at all, they've got the wrong crossroads."

"Well, that adds insult to injury," said Mum indignantly.

Grampy Farmbrough gave a knowing smile, took his pipe from his mouth, and said:

"That might not be such a bad thing, let's look at it this way, we don't need any more notoriety, do we?"

17

Sayings and Superstitions

As we were growing up at Finchers, Primrose Hill, we overheard and observed a lot of strange sayings and superstitions – few of them made sense to us children – but these rituals were absorbed into our everyday existence. Today, most of them have disappeared from use; however, these experiences from our childhood linger in the memory and are verbal links to the generations long-gone.

Sayings:
It's looking a bit black over our Will's mother's. (About the weather.)
It's in Annie's room behind the clock. (When you're not meant to find something that's lost.) I often wondered if there was a little door behind the clock on the mantelpiece, leading to Annie's room.
Look after the pennies, and the pounds'll take care of themselves. (Don't waste money on trivial items.) But where were the pounds?
If the Lord don't come, he sends. (When some good fortune turns up.)
Give him an inch and he'll take a mile. (About someone who will take advantage of any circumstance.)
A nod is as good as a wink. (About an implied suggestion.) Sometimes extended with **to a blind man.** (When someone who continues regardless of advice.)

He could go on until the cows come home. (When the speaker doesn't know when to stop.)

Superstitions:
Crossed knives on the table. Signifying trouble or bad luck.
Cover the mirror and silver in a thunderstorm. The first cloth to hand should be used: tea towel, cardigan, scarf – otherwise explosions or worse could happen.
Spill salt, spill sorrow. Followed by taking a pinch of spilt salt and throwing it over left shoulder, to undo the sorrow.
Broken mirror. Seven years' bad luck.
Never do washing on Good Friday. You could wash away a loved one.
Don't put new shoes on the table. A sign of death or tragedy in the family.
A pinch and a punch on the first of the month. To bring good luck: the first greeting to anyone on the first day of each month, a great favourite with the boys at school.
Never open an umbrella indoors. An omen of tragedy or bad luck.

18

Keeping Warm

When our parents bought Finchers in 1945 it was in a poor, neglected state. The bungalow had been built between the wars, and in the kitchen the original cast-iron stove had an open hearth, with a small oven above and a back boiler for hot water. This stove was very inefficient, it burnt up all the fuel without putting out any heat. On the far side of the kitchen was an electric cooker and an electric kettle which Mum and Dad had saved up for and bought to supplement the stove, but these were useless in power cuts.

In 1947 the bitterly cold weather and blizzards affected the whole country and went on for weeks. The bad weather was so severe it disrupted the train network and coal was prevented from reaching the power stations causing widespread power cuts.

It was so cold; people wore their overcoats and gloves indoors to keep warm. Nearly all the children we knew had chilblains on their toes (and sometimes legs as well) that throbbed and itched as soon as we got warm.

During the power cuts of 1947, factories had to close or work short time. Even when Dad was able to work, he sometimes returned at the end of the day to a cold home, the kitchen lit by candles and his meal warming over a small oil stove.

One day Dad said:

"This just won't do. These power cuts are draining the life out of us ordinary folk. I hate to see us living like this."

Mum was at her wits' end:

"I'm so sorry, I just don't know what to do. I would dearly love to have a warm kitchen and proper meal ready for you when you get home, but try as I might, I just can't get any heat from this old stove."

Dad put his arm round Mum's shoulder:

"It's not your fault Sybil, you're a great cook; you just need the right tools for the job."

Later, when they had cleared away and washed up, Dad said:

"Next time we can get to Wycombe, we'll have a look round. I've heard these new enamelled cast-iron stoves are far more efficient."

Mum's eyes lit up:

"Just imagine that, and a new stove might be easier to clean."

And that's how F.W. George, the heating engineers, came and removed the old stove and transformed the kitchen with a new stove made by Courtier.

It was solid and cream coloured. It used coke in a fire to one side that could be banked up and the door closed, to stay in overnight. There was a large oven on the other side and a hot plate along the top with drop-down insulated heat preservers.

"Hot porridge girls! Come and get it."

At breakfast time Mum was standing at the Courtier, stirring the saucepan; and we children loved it, we could dress and undress in front of the stove and warm our clothes on the towel rail in front. In those days we wore a woollen vest and a liberty bodice under our viyella blouses. At night our hot-water bottles were filled from the kettle on the hob.

On baking day, taking a cake out of the Courtier oven, Mum exclaimed:

"Girls, look at this cake, it's baked all the way through, and it's got a lovely crack across the top!"

Finchers had a second fireplace in the front room but fuel was expensive, so although the front room was used in the summer for Sunday afternoon tea and card or board games afterwards, during the winter we didn't use the room, or light the fire except for birthdays and at Christmas.

All this had to change once we got a television in time for the Coronation on the second of June 1953 and it was installed in the front room to one side of the fireplace.

Although not allowed to touch the television set, Mary and I soon became familiar with terms like "tuning in" and "horizontal and vertical line hold". Once the picture had settled down, we were able to follow children's serials like *The Railway Children*, *Heidi* and *Anne of Green Gables*. Previously, we had found it difficult to follow a story from Uncle Mac on the wireless, but now, on the television, it was so easy to see and hear each gripping episode as the stories unfolded. Mum watched with us; she enjoyed a good story.

Until 1955, there was only one television channel, which was transmitted by the BBC. The Postmaster General controlled the weekly permitted hours of transmission. Children's television was on for an hour a day between five and six o'clock in the evening, and adult television for two hours between eight and ten o'clock. At the weekends up to eight hours a day were allowed. Before each transmission there was a "signal" to allow viewers time to tune in.

The evening programmes started with an image on the screen depicting the word "*Newsreel*" rotating round the top of the transmitter at Alexandra Palace, followed by a short news programme. On Friday nights our parents watched *Café Continental*; other programmes they liked were *Panorama* (which started in November 1953) and plays from the *Armchair Theatre* or films such as *The Quatermass Experiment*. At the weekends we watched live outside broadcasts like *The International Horse Show* from White City, and Dad liked *Motor Racing from Silverstone*.

An annual highlight of weekend live television was *The University Boat Race* which brought out a competitive spirit in our family. Dad and I were for Oxford and Mum and Mary for Cambridge. Relying on the commentary, we watched the tiny screen and shouted encouragement to our respective teams or were horror-struck when one of the boats sank. The penalty for our losing team was to buy a box of sweets from Manning's Post Office at Hazlemere crossroads.

As the days shortened the temperature in the front room dropped, soon it was time to light the fire, but only at the weekends when our parents would go into the front room to watch the television in the evenings. On weekdays they stayed in the kitchen and listened to the wireless.

Mum would light the fire; kneeling to use a match, she would sit back on her heels to see if the fire would "draw". If the wind was in the wrong direction the flames could easily flicker and die; the remedy was to take several sheets of newspaper and hold these across the front of the fire to encourage the air through the grate, this usually did the trick.

Once, when the chimney needed sweeping, and the newspaper was not removed quickly enough, we heard a rushing, roaring sound and saw flames leaping through the newspaper and up the chimney.

In a panic Mum jumped up:

"Oh no! The chimney's on fire!"

"Quickly, Diana, get the salt from the kitchen to sprinkle over the fire."

"I'll go and fetch a wet sack."

"There's no time to lose or the house'll catch fire!"

Grabbing the salt drum, I rushed back to throw handfuls on to the flames and, as I looked up the chimney, I saw soot glowing bright red. In no time Mum came back with a sack soaking in our washing-up bowl; she stuffed it up the chimney to block out any air.

"What'll we do if the house burns down?" asked Mary.

"I don't know, let's hope the sack works!" I said.

We waited an age until the mighty roaring sound slowly subsided, then Mum heaved a sigh of relief, and said:

"Thank goodness that's over, it could have been much worse."

"We'd better clear up this mess before Dad gets home. We won't be having any more fires in here until the sweep's been. I'll write to him and get Dad to put the letter through his door."

Joey, our budgerigar, who had been squawking and flapping in his cage on top of the bookcase throughout the whole crisis, settled back on his perch.

On chimney sweeping day, preparations included moving furniture away from the fireplace and rolling the carpet back. On one occasion,

18.1 Waiting for the sweep's brush
Mary, Diana and cousin Alan Barker.

Alan Barker was staying with us because his mum, our Aunty Ruby, had recently died. Mum's tactic to keep us children out of the sweep's way was to encourage us to look for his brush coming out the top of the chimney.

"Which chimney will the brush come out of?" asked Alan.

"He always does the kitchen first, that's the back chimney – and there it is!" I exclaimed.

It was a flat round brush, attached to a thin pole; it appeared and disappeared and then reappeared, and we laughed because we could hear the sweep calling:

"Can you see it yet?"

The sweep moved into the front room and repeated his brushing. At last, both chimneys were swept.

"Now we must give the room a good cleaning from top to bottom." Mum was practical as ever, a signal for us children to go and play in the road.

Besides the kitchen and front room, there were three other rooms in our bungalow, two bedrooms and the bathroom. None of them had a fireplace and in the worst weather other forms of heating were needed.

In their bedroom our parents used a single bar electric fire, a safety hazard that would not be permitted in today's world. Heating was especially necessary when our father suffered one of his recurring bouts of chronic bronchitis and spent days on end in bed. Antibiotics were not yet readily available.

In our bedroom, Mary and I had an Aladdin radiator. When we drove to visit our cousins at Wood Green, we went past the Aladdin factory on the Western Avenue. On the top of the factory was a red glowing lantern, so we knew it was associated with a story from the Arabian Nights!

Our radiator gave off a distinctive chemical smell that wasn't unpleasant. The oilman came to fill a large drum that was standing on bricks in the shed. There was a tap at the bottom from which Mum drew off enough paraffin to fill the radiator reservoir. Then she would remove the glass funnel, trim the wick, and light the flame. The reservoir fitted behind the drop-down flap at the base of the radiator.

On Friday, bath and hair washing night, the radiator was moved into the bathroom to take the chill off. Mary and I shared the bath until neither of us wanted to sit on the plug. Even with the radiator, the bathroom was still chilly and as soon as we were out of the bath, we dashed into the kitchen wrapped in our bath towels, to dry off in front of the fire before putting on our nightclothes. The radiator would then be carried carefully back to our bedroom in time for bed.

Mary and I knew it was dangerous to touch it or put anything on the radiator, but after a bedtime story and being tucked up for the night, we found the light from the blue flame playing on our bedroom walls and ceiling very reassuring. The radiator would be extinguished by our parents after we were asleep. We didn't realise at the time that the radiator produced a great deal of condensation as it burned, and many a morning we would draw back our bedroom curtains to find the condensation frozen and the windows covered with the most beautiful patterns of ice, swirling across the panes of glass.

Before central heating every winter presented a constant challenge of how to keep warm, our parents were not alone in facing the problem of how to make winter bearable. Now, seventy years on, I really appreciate the luxury of living in a warm and comfortable home.

19

Grampy Farmbrough Makes Tea at The Coppice

High on the mantelpiece, the black marble clock, looking like a tiny Palladian villa, strikes four.

Grandfather, being a man of habit and ritual, rises from his fireside chair and says:

"Kettle's boiling, tea in pot, this reviver beats the lot. Who's for a cuppa?"[*]

Our parents nod assent, then quickly add,

"But we won't eat, we've tea ready at Finchers."

The teapot is already warming by the open fire on the hob opposite the kettle, grandfather carefully measures six spoons of leaves and replaces the caddy on the mantel. Using a potholder, he adds boiling water, and moves the pot to a wooden stand on the table in the middle of the room.

Half the table is laid with a linen cloth from the dresser, and on it pretty cups, saucers and plates, sugar, honey; the breadboard with a freshly baked cottage loaf in a white paper bag, with red lettering:

G. Lester's Park Lane

Knives and spoons from the sideboard, milk and butter from the pantry by the scullery complete the scene. On cue Uncle appears from

---

[*] *(We always thought Grampy said: "Kettle's boiling, tea in pot, Mrs Ivor drinks the lot" – but we weren't sure who Mrs Ivor was).*

the garden, looking dishevelled and sunburnt, he greets his brother and family:

"B'aint 'alf bad."

The old man does everything with care and precision, having lost the tops from his index and middle fingers on both hands, a legacy from many years in the High Wycombe furniture industry.

Standing at the head of the table, grandfather adds milk to the cups and pours the tea – it comes out thick and strong. He adds sugar by the spoonful to order, and passes the drinks round. He pulls the knot from the top of the cottage loaf and holding it against his body, he uses the breadknife to remove a crust, then, buttering as he goes, cuts two more slices. The new bread smells good. By the time the buttered slices are spread with heather honey, we children are drooling in anticipation. Eventually he concedes and cuts a slice in half for us to share.

In doing so, he gives us not only a taste of new bread, butter and honey, but also a memory that will resonate through the years; long after the adults in the room are dead and the house gone.

These mingled smells and flavours will evoke that room, that time, the woodsmoke from the open fire, the clock ticking on the mantelpiece, the stuffed badger's head and riding crop hanging on the wall, dust dancing in the shafts of sunlight playing through the window, the table set for tea and a wonderful sense of being present and belonging.

20

Going to Wycombe

20.1 Market day, High Street, High Wycombe (looking east)

When we lived at Primrose Hill, going shopping in High Wycombe was not something we did very often. The rural isolation and lack of transport dictated that daily necessities, bread, milk and groceries, were brought to the house. Mum was a good needlewoman and she made our dresses and knitted jumpers and cardigans; in those days everyone had to make do and mend. "Going to Wycombe" usually involved an expedition to the library, dentist, optician, bank or to buy clothing that Mum couldn't make.

One Saturday morning in early April 1952, Mum said we needed new school uniforms for the summer. I was due a regular eye test, so we would go to the optician first, walk along the market and do a bit of shopping before we met Dad when he finished work. He would come with us to buy new sandals and blazers for the summer term.

We boarded the 9 o'clock bus at the bottom of Primrose Hill, this was the terminus and the bus was empty. Mary and I always tried to persuade Mum to sit upstairs because we liked to look over the hedges, but she was adamant:

"You know I don't like the cigarette smoke upstairs, and keep away from those side seats, they are too near the door: there's nowhere to hold on to when the bus goes round a corner." So as usual, we went to the front and sat looking at the road ahead, and Mum sat behind us. The driver, who had been chatting to the conductor outside at the front of the bus, climbed up into his cab and the conductor mounted the rear platform and came down to the front to collect our fares.

"One and two halves to Wycombe, please," asked Mum.

"That'll be seven pence."

The coloured cardboard tickets were held on a wooden rack and were printed and ranked by denomination, the conductor punched a hole in each ticket before he gave them to us, and he put the money in his satchel.

The route wound up Brimmers Hill, past Lorely, the home of our cousins Molly and Alan Barker. We stopped to pick up passengers at Widmer End, some of whom Mum knew from the Young Wives' Group, so she passed the time of day with them. There were other stops on the way through Four Ashes, and Terriers, by this time some older children had got on looking forward to Saturday morning cinema at the Odeon, and the bus was getting noisy with their chatter. The bus went down Amersham Hill, over the railway bridge and into High Wycombe.

At the Crendon Street stop, the children going to the cinema rushed to get off and as we were furthest from the platform, Mum said:

"We'd better hold back and let them go first."

We crossed over to Hamblin's for my eye test. The interior felt intimidating and very quiet: we spoke with hushed voices. We were taken into a dark room and the optician placed heavy metal frames on my nose and asked me to read the illuminated letters on the opposite side of the room. He had a large flat tray of round lenses arranged in rows; he sorted through them and tried various combinations in the frames, which became increasingly heavy. He asked me:

"Which is better, this one or this one?"

I was in a quandary; it was very difficult to say which was the clearer; with one lens the image appeared further away but not clearer. I wondered how best to please the optician, so I said:

"I'm not sure."

Eventually Mum was told that I needed stronger lenses in new National Health Service frames. Measurements were taken and we were asked to come back in three weeks' time.

After Hamblin's, we walked down Crendon Street, and as we passed the door of Mr. Gibb our dentist, it sent a shiver of apprehension through us: how glad we were that we could walk past. Just sitting in his waiting room filled us with fear and trepidation. His chairside manner only made matters worse: "Sit still and stop wriggling – the more you move, the more it will hurt."

At the traffic lights we turned into the High Street, the main A40 trunk road from London to Oxford – it was very busy with traffic. The market, set up along the sunny side of the High Street, was very popular and crowded with people who jostled along the pavement in both directions. It was a mass of colours and sounds, the vegetable stalls set out with arrays of potatoes, carrots, cabbages and celery, and the fruit stalls displaying precisely aligned piles of produce, green and red apples, oranges, lemons and grapefruit. The fruit stallholder called out loudly in a sing-song cockney voice:

"Apples thru'pence a pa'arnd… pears."

At a flower stall, a mass of yellow daffodils, white narcissus with orange centres, tulips of all colours and sprays of mimosa, Mum caught sight of an exotic spray of orchids wrapped in cellophane and explained wistfully:

"These are what ladies wear as a corsage on their evening dresses, for a grand night out."

Mary and I looked at them; they didn't seem very special to us, in fact a bit gaudy, so Mary said:

"Wouldn't a rose look just as good?" and Mum agreed.

One of Mum's favourites was the fabric stall, piled high with bolts of cloth, some draped up and over the sides of the stall:

"All good quality stuff, best tweed and cotton."

Mum took care to select the most suitable fabric at a reasonable price. She chose blue gingham for our school dresses; three yards were measured and mum paid the stall holder.

Halfway along the High Street we visited David Greig, the grocer. Just inside the two front doors was the cashier's desk, marble-topped counters were arranged round the other three sides. The floor was chequered with dark red and white tiles, on the walls the white tiles had a distinctive frieze of green and purple thistles. Mum bought fresh ground coffee and Wensleydale cheese and she gave me the sales slips and some coins because I was small enough and old enough to weave between the customers waiting to be served. I went to the cashier, who took the money and receipted the slips and I threaded my way back to Mum. She then exchanged the receipted slips for the coffee and cheese.

Our next stop was the Trustee Savings Bank in Church Street. Mary and I looked wearily at each other; we knew that the long queue meant our legs would be aching before Mum was served. In her handbag Mum had our National Savings Stamp Books and our individual TSB account books. At last Mum reached the high counter and in the dim, cream glow she handed over each bank book with the savings stamps tucked inside. The bank clerk entered the new total by hand and returned them to Mum – she looked very pleased as she slipped them back into her handbag, saying:

"Well, that all adds to your savings for when you go to the High School."

Next door to the bank was Lyons Tea Shop. As we entered, the welcome warmth of the cream and green restaurant wrapped round us. We walked past the front counter and into the seating area at the back.

With our tray we made for the steaming tea urn, where a jolly lady in a Lyons uniform and frilled hat said:

"'ello luv, what can I get you today?"

Mum replied:

"Two cups of tea, one with extra milk, an extra cup, and two tea cakes, please."

The tea lady poured the tea and collected the tea cakes:

"That'll be eleven pence luv; the knives and spoons are just over there."

Glad to sit down at last, Mum poured half the milky tea into the spare cup, Mary and I were used to sharing a cup of tea, but we made sure the second tea cake was cut vertically because neither of us wanted the bottom portion. We carefully spread our helping with butter and tucked in. The tearoom was busy and there was a low mumble of conversation from customers on the other tables; we looked round, and wondered whether they too were having a treat like us, or did they drink tea there every day? Seeing us staring and being nosy, Mum said:

"We had better get a move on. Hurry up and finish your drinks, or we won't be in time to meet Dad when he finishes work."

Next stop was Woolworths, an L-shaped shop. We entered from Church Street, and we were going to leave by the Frogmoor exit. This was another dimly lit shop, the dark wooden counters had high glass fronts held together with chromium clips. It was always crowded with customers; there was a lot of noise from voices and tills ringing, and it was easy to get lost – always a frightening prospect.

Our instructions in that event were to make our way to the Church Street entrance where there was a large weighing machine; we should look over the tops of people's heads for the big red dial that showed people's weight, then stand on the platform and wait for Mum. It was a squeeze to get round the shop, we kept close to Mum; she bought some buttons for our new dresses and batteries for our torches. We finally emerged on to Frogmoor, and stood on the edge of the pavement, excited to be looking for Dad with the car.

Equally pleased to be meeting us and to be taking his family on a spending spree, Dad had cleaned up from work and slipped on his sports jacket. Mum put her shopping basket in the back of the car and

20.2 Frogmoor, High Wycombe

then we were free to go to John Hearn's Shoe Shop on the corner of
Frogmoor and Oxford Road.

"We want brown T-bar sandals for school," Mum said to the shop
assistant.

My heart sank, and I tried to compromise:

"Oh! Do I have to have the brown ones, the red ones are really
lovely?"

This was why Dad came with us, as he reminded us:

"You both need sensible sandals for the summer."

The shop assistant looked at me sympathetically:

"Why not try on these Clarks sandals and we can look in the X-ray
machine* to make sure they are a good fit."

As we left the shop Dad thought he ought to warn us:

"You've got to make these sandals last. Take them off when you get
home from school, and don't play in them."

Clutching our boxes of new sandals, we made our way down
White Hart Street, walking through the bustle of people in the New

---

* *During the 1950s X-ray machines in shoe shops were very popular. Sometimes called
"pedoscope", they enabled the viewer to see the bones of the feet inside the shoe. Although
the dangers of X-rays were well known, perhaps because the effects of radiation emerged
slowly, the connection with these foot machines was overlooked, and they were not phased
out until the 1970s.*

Market at the corner with Paul's Row, and past one of Dad's favourite stalls selling tools and engineering equipment. The stallholder always called out:

"I sell surplus and bankrupt stock." Dad sometimes had a word with him, but this time he just looked, and we kept going.

We walked through the market stalls under the colonnaded Guildhall, and just beyond reached the Co-op. School uniforms were on the first floor, where we made our way to a row of navy blue blazers. Mum sorted through them:

"Try this on, it looks about your size. I need to make sure there's plenty of room over the shoulders." Mary had only just started in the "Big School" and this was her first blazer – usually she couldn't wear my cast-offs because we were almost the same size, despite the age difference. We both felt smothered in the blazers we tried on, either too long in the body or arms. Eventually we both found blazers to fit.

"Just look at these prices, anyone would think I'm made of money," said Dad.

The sales assistant asked for our Co-op Dividend number, she then put the sales slip and cash into a cylinder and twisted to close it. With a loud whoosh, the cylinder was whisked away by a vacuum tube system to a central cashier behind the scenes. The receipt and change came back in the same cylinder and dropped into a tray on the counter. By that time the sales assistant had wrapped the blazers and tied the parcel with string.

"I suppose the best way to look at it is that we shall get the 'Divi' at the end of the year," said Dad.

Our shopping expedition was over; Dad went to get the car from Frogmoor and we crossed over to the other side of the High Street, where he would pick us up and drive us home for a late dinner.

Mum found one last pleasure from the outing. Before sitting down to our meal, she had filled the coffee percolator and as we ate, the deep aroma of fresh coffee filled the kitchen. Afterwards, she and Dad sat back and enjoyed a cup of the freshly percolated coffee, purchased from Greig's that morning.

21

I Used To Be Quite Famous You Know

21.1 The Primrose Hill gang
Diana, Mary, Susan and Jimmy Bennell

When we were growing up in rural Buckinghamshire in the 1950s, it was quite a common sight to see the children at Primrose Hill playing together in the road. Weather permitting, we would be marking out a hopscotch grid with chalk from our gardens, skipping, playing conkers, marbles or just messing about, especially if there was work going on in one of the nearby fields for us to watch.

Mum was quite relaxed about this. Little did she know that if we wandered up the road, away from the houses, we were tempted into more risky behaviour, such as scrumping pears from an overhanging tree in Farmer Stephens' garden or experimenting smoking a cigarette one of the boys had found in a discarded packet. We occasionally strayed down footpaths and then had to race home, nearly late. Mum was relying on the lack of traffic to keep us safe; it meant she could get on with her housework in the mornings or sewing in the afternoons. If we went into a neighbours' garden, she always wanted to know whose, and to make sure that we would be home for mealtimes. She would regularly remind us of the dangers of talking to travellers, rag-and-bone men… and old Mrs. Green.

Old Mrs. Green was the recluse who lived in a small wooden shack behind a high hedge at the top of the road. We tried not to stare but were in awe that in all weathers she wore an old fur coat, fur boots and felt hat and carried a tattered leather handbag.

On her return from the village, we could hear her talking to herself, whilst carrying her string shopping bag with scraps from the fish shop wrapped in newspaper. She would be gazing solidly at the road in front of her and we could see her dirt-engrained hands, thick make-up and haphazard red lipstick. The effect was quite frightening.

The Primrose Hill gang comprised the Bennell family: Susan (a bit older than Mary and me), Jimmy (a bit younger) and Johnny (younger still) – the two Bennell boys had bright red hair; Alan Tilly, an only child, whose mother used to send him out dressed immaculately whatever the occasion; Mary and me; and sometimes Keith Pearce, the youngest of a large family, but older than any of us.

One day when the gang had wandered to the top of the road, Keith Pearce said:

"Can you smell that pong of fish? I dare you to look through old Mrs Green's gateway and see if she's at home."

I peered round the corner of the hedge looking towards the wooden shed.

"Her doorstep's full of saucers and dishes."

"That's for all the stray cats she feeds."

Then there was a noise from inside, and we got scared and ran back down the road.

That evening as it was getting dark, just before Dad came home, Mum went to draw the kitchen curtains and got a nasty shock: there was Mrs. Green's ghastly face pressed up against the windowpane and staring in.

Mum shrieked:

"Go away, you dirty old woman." And she did go away, but she left us upset and crying.

As soon as Dad came home and heard what had happened, he jumped straight back on his motorbike and went up to see Mrs. Green. He was away for quite some time and when he did return, he gathered Mary and me on his knee:

"Well, it's a sad old story, and I don't rightly know whether I should be telling you all this," he said.

"Oh dear, what's sad? Please tell us," we begged.

"Well, evidently Mrs. Green used to be quite well known; her husband was Mayor of High Wycombe and they were always going to civic functions and the like. She had her picture in the *Bucks Free Press* a lot."

"D'you know, I thought she looked familiar," said Mum.

Then Dad continued:

"She had a bad time during the war, lost her husband, children and home. She says she came to Primrose Hill looking for a bit of peace and quiet."

"Oh dear, what happened to her children?" we asked, feeling sorry and concerned at what happened.

"She didn't say, but although people say she's not right in the head, she says she needs time to get back on an even keel and to be left alone with her cats."

"Will she come and look in our window again?" we wondered.

"I don't think you need worry about that; but now you know her story, perhaps you will see her differently?"

Soon after, Dad gave us both a hug and tucked us up in bed; reassured and trusting Dad, we dropped off to sleep.

The next day we told our friends what had happened and we all felt sorry for Mrs Green but had no idea how to react towards her. Life on Primrose Hill went on as usual. In those days there were no social services or housing officers to deal with such problems.

Mrs Green still walked past us from time to time in her old fur coat get-up, on the way to the fish shop, and we children continued to watch her with uneasy fascination, and she continued to ignore us, talking to herself all the time. Perhaps she was answering a deep need in us by providing something for us to be frightened of.

22

The River Thames

Is it really so strange that a body of water can exert an influence over the people who live near it or come into contact with it, a presence that can transcend the generations?

The River Thames was only six miles from where I grew up near High Wycombe in the Chiltern Hills, and as soon as my parents bought their first car in 1949, it was almost inevitable that for Sunday afternoon jaunts, we would head to the river. After all, children and water are a winning combination.

Our nearest access to the river was at Marlow, where the Compleat Angler Hotel nestled beside a remarkable suspension bridge (with a two-ton weight limit). At Marlow there were walks along the towpath in either direction. However, because it was a town, my sister and I were not allowed to paddle or do anything unseemly. So, Marlow was reserved for short winter walks and a memorable concert of Handel's Water Music performed from a barge moored alongside the towpath.

One of my early memories is of a happy sunny afternoon by the river at Medmenham. The hay had just been cut and was still drying; we children played at gathering it up and making dens. After tiring of that, we found a gap between the reeds on the riverbank where there was a small beach of sandy silt,

"Let's go paddling!"

"If you want to go in the water, let's take your sandals and socks off first," said Mum. "We had better tuck your dress into your knickers before it gets wet."

22.1 Mary, Diana and Geoffrey playing in the hay at Medmenham

And so, we paddled and splashed, savouring the cool clear water, screaming with mock horror and delight.

Many of these outings were shared with Pauline, Reg, and our cousin Geoffrey; locations along the river between Marlow and Henley were found and we picnicked at Hurley, Bisham, Hambleden and Temple. In those days, after haymaking in June, the trusting farmers would leave their fields ungated and access to the river was assured. But abuse of this trust and hospitality ensured the practice disappeared in a matter of years.

"Better get the kettle on," cried Dad.

Our family picnics required that at four o'clock our father would take out his trusty primus stove and home-made collapsible windbreak to boil a kettle and make tea. Milk was brought in a medicine bottle with a cork stopper. Mum produced egg or jam sandwiches and a piece of fruit cake. After tea there was just time for a quick game of bat and ball:

"It's my bat, I'm in first."

"I caught you out, it's my turn."

"It's not fair, I never get a turn."

Then we all piled back into the car for the journey home: sunburnt and itchy from the hay, but very tired and happy.

For our father and his sister these river picnics must have evoked memories of their own childhood. They were eighth and ninth of a family of ten with limited means. Their annual holiday was restricted to a day trip by train to the River Thames at Bourne End, by all accounts a happy and carefree adventure. Who is to say, when it came to a choice of picnic locations, whether the river was exerting a subconscious pressure on their choice?

As a family, we were drawn to the River Thames in other ways at different times of the year. Where a river is navigable locks and weirs are needed to control the height and flow of the water. We found it interesting and educational to watch pleasure boats negotiating a lock. At times when restricted by our father's ill health, he and Mum would be very content to sit and watch the antics of boat owners as they negotiated a lock. The lock keeper would generally welcome help with

22.2 The Farmbrough family's day out at Bourne End
(Connie, Pauline, Ruby, neighbour Ted, Phyl, Pete)

the heavy lock gates, so my sister Mary and I would join in opening the gates at one end to allow boats in, then wait while the height of the water rose or fell according to the direction of travel, before the gates at the opposite end were opened to allow the craft out of the lock to continue their journey.

Some of the boat owners and crew found the whole process very disconcerting, particularly if there was a sudden rise or fall of their vessel. More than once a crew member on the lock side holding a rope would be stranded and obliged to run along the riverbank to be reunited with his boat.

"You'll just have to let go of that rope, run across the lock, and I'll wait for you where I can, further along…"

"What do you mean, you can't run?"

Visiting locks obviously filled the need for a good outing with minimal financial outlay. Our parents would seek out various locks along the river, a favourite being Boulters Lock at Ray Mill Island, Maidenhead, because it was a busy lock and it had a large accessible car park. We also visited locks at Dorney and Boveney near Windsor. From Boveney the river flows in a long arc around Windsor Castle, leaving only the southern side of the castle with a land boundary.

Was the river exerting its influence again, but this time on our mother, who was born by the River Thames at Whitton? She knew that her grandfather had worked at Home Farm on the Windsor Estate, that her grandmother had worked for a master at Eton College; also, that her mother, Lily, was born in the shadow of Windsor Castle. Were subconscious ties or longings pulling her back to the places that held a special affinity for her family?

The River Thames is a permanent but fluid feature of the landscape, with an energy of its own, reminding us that like time, it is always moving. The river has a long history: artefacts have been found dating from Neolithic times. The Romans built a city where the river was deep but sufficiently narrow to bridge. That city is now called London.

Along its 215 miles, the Thames, with its restless moods, will influence the lives of countless inhabitants of the many towns, villages and hamlets it flows through. In 1929 the MP John Burns described the Thames as *liquid history*; if this is true at national level, it must equally apply to the lives of the ordinary people and their descendants.

23

A Day in the Life of Grampy Farmbrough

We visited Grampy Farmbrough most weeks, usually after Sunday School. Running up the front path of The Coppice, my sister and I would round the corner into the backyard and often find him on the garden seat against the south-facing wall of the brick shed, soaking up the sun.

He was a tall, angular man with sparse grey hair, usually covered with his cloth cap. His skin was wrinkled and tanned from the sun. He was always smartly dressed in a waistcoat, collar and tie. His boots were always well polished, and when not on his feet, would be warming, heels on the fender, by the fire in the kitchen. He loved his roses and, when in bloom, he would sport a rosebud in his buttonhole.

"Sometimes I sits and thinks, and sometimes I just sits," he would say.

By the time my sister and I were born our grandfather was in his late sixties and retired after many years working in the furniture industry. We never knew his wife (our grandmother), Sarah Ellen Mines, who died when our father was twelve years old. We never knew Grampy as a breadwinner for his ten children, nor as a gardener, an allotment holder or as a pig, goat and beekeeper. He occasionally referred to his beekeeping days:

"All those bee stings over the years, that's what keeps the rheumatics away."

To us Grampy was very old and, apparently, a man of leisure. He was able to maintain this illusion and, in doing so, his place at the head of the family because his daughters – Win, Marj, Ruby, Pauline and Connie – called at The Coppice on their appointed day and time to cook, clean, take the washing or do the shopping and, between them, keep the household (Grampy, Uncle David and Scamp) functioning smoothly. Our mother baked pies or cakes and in exchange we all received vegetables grown by Uncle David:

"Here's some parsnips, and a savoy. I'll just wrap 'em in a few sheets of newspaper."

By the end of each week, Grampy had received and disseminated news from most of the family. He was a communications hub:

"I hear Dennis (Uncle Jack's oldest son) has signed up for the Royal Marines."

Uncle Jack came, but only to do wood turning in the woodshed, not to help with the chores.

Only one member of his family had a telephone, and that was his daughter Phyl who married her cousin Reg (Grampy's nephew). They lived in London with our cousins Michael and Renee. Grampy could ring Phyl when necessary, by using the phone of Mr. Hearne, the coalman, three doors up on Holmer Green Road.

The lack of a phone at Primrose Hill was overcome by Mr. White, the Special Constable, who permitted us to call Aunty Phyl. We felt very important holding the earpiece to our ears and talking into the upright speaker:

"Wood Green 6779 please."

The telephonist, using her refined voice, would reply:

"One moment please while I try to connect you."

Grampy was not one to spend money unnecessarily; when, during the 1950s, the Council said The Coppice should have an inside lavatory and cesspool, he went along with all the upheaval, installing the lavatory and digging trenches and pit for the cesspool – but before it was brought into use, he sent someone down to knock a hole in the bottom of the cesspool, thus ensuring it never needed to be emptied, and saving him the regular expense.

Grampy liked to tell the story about the first time he went to the pictures (cinema). It was so dark; he followed the circle of light on the floor from the usherette's torch and found a seat. "The film was good and I could hear every word, but I thought the seats were a bit narrow and uncomfortable," he said. It turned out he had watched the whole film perched on the top edge of the seat, because no one had told him that the seats folded down.

Grampy Farmbrough was a familiar face in Hazlemere, and being a man of habit and ritual, he did things at the same time on the same days. On Thursdays just before mid-day, he and Scamp would walk up to the Post Office at the crossroads to collect his pension. Scamp would wait patiently as Mr. Manning, the postmaster, counted out the money and a few courteous remarks were exchanged:

"It's nice to see a bit of sunshine for a change, Mr. Farmbrough."

And Grampy would reply:

"I see your Norman's not in the shop today, I hope he's well?"

From the Post Office Grampy and Scamp would turn left and walk along Amersham Road as far as the Queen's Head for a half pint of beer and to pay the slate club* dues. After leaving the pub, their next stop was at Lester's Grocers in Park Lane, where Grampy would settle up the grocery bill for the week. Finally, it was only a short walk home to The Coppice for something to eat followed by a nap in the sun.

Grampy could sight-read music and was a long-standing member of the Hazlemere Church Choir. He attended choir practice on a weekday evening and two services on Sunday. On each occasion he would walk to the church but before returning home after choir practice and evensong, he would join other choristers in The Crown opposite the church for a half pint. This he always referred to as:

"Thirsting after righteousness."

When we were in the congregation on Sunday mornings, we looked to see if Grampy turned off his hearing aid as the sermon started. He claimed this was to save the battery, but we suspected other motives and were envious.

Grampy walked with a stick; when he caught sight of someone he knew, he would raise his stick to a forty-five-degree angle and nod his head in acknowledgement, rather than call out a greeting. Our

---

* *The slate club was a thrift society for emergency relief and Christmas*

Dad and his brothers thought this was amusing and called him "Wag" behind his back; they would never dare to tell him to his face.

When the mobile library began visiting Hazlemere, it called at Park Lane and Grampy became a regular member. His favourite author was Leslie Charteris and he worked his way avidly through a series about Simon Templar (alias *The Saint,* whose calling card was a stick figure crowned with a halo), who was a criminal turned detective. Grampy would tell us about his latest thrilling adventure exposing corrupt politicians and officials. As only about fifty books in *The Saint* series were published in the United Kingdom, we noticed over the years that Grampy was happily re-reading the same stories, with equal enjoyment.

In the early autumn, Grampy used his love of roses as an excuse to call on each of his children living within Vespa distance. He would park his moped at the front gate, and taking out his secateurs, prune the front garden roses before announcing his visit. Our mother found this a most annoying habit: she too loved her roses; she was waiting for the last rose of summer and was keen to fill her rose bowl once more, but as we walked down the path to see him off, we saw the look of horror on her face as she caught sight of her beloved rose trees reduced to a few bare sticks. Our aunts and uncles exchanged commiserations:

"Has he done yer roses yet?" and "Well, that's the end of the roses for another year then."

Grampy could play the piano or harmonium by ear, and on occasions when he came out for a ride in the car on a Sunday afternoon, we would often end up near Dinton, in the Vale of Aylesbury, or visit almost any church that happened to be open. Going inside the church, he would sit down at the harmonium, pedal the bellows and, even with his shortened fingers, pick out a well-know-hymn such as "Nearer My God, to Thee" or "The Day Thou Gavest, Lord, Is Ended".

24

All in the Family

Our cousin, Renee, lived with her parents, Aunty Phyl and Uncle Reg, and her brother, Michael, at Wood Green in north London, but because of two evacuations to Hazlemere during the war, when strong ties with her Hazlemere cousins were formed, she became an important part of our family circle as we grew up after the war. Renee was seven years older than me and in many ways a role model; she epitomised what Mary and I hoped to become. Her visits during the school holidays were full of fun, and new games brought with her from London. She was good at fuelling our imaginations by showing us how to make mossy fairy rings and beds for the fairies, and the next morning to discover the fairies had been and left their beds unmade. Another time she borrowed our mother's bicycle so the three of us could pedal round the local lanes, with Mary working extra hard, still on her tricycle. If Renee happened to visit over a weekend, there were family picnics. On one occasion, we were setting up our picnic in a bluebell wood near Hampden, when suddenly there was a flash of lightning and rumble of thunder. To Renee's dismay, our parents hastily packed up the picnic and drove us home. Not to be deprived of the treat, once back home, the tablecloth and picnic were set out on the front room carpet; and as we sat cross-legged on the floor, Renee said:

"Let's pretend we are still surrounded by bluebells! There's some blue in the carpet, perhaps they could be our bluebells?"

Mum and Dad laughed but Mary and I mimed picking the flowers.

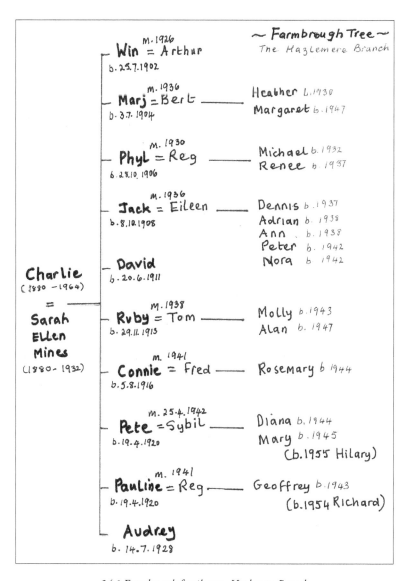

~ Farmbrough Tree ~
The Hazlemere Branch

Win = Arthur
m. 1926
b. 25.7.1902

Marj = Bert
m. 1936
b. 3.7. 1904
Heather b.1930
Margaret b.1947

Phyl = Reg
m. 1930
b. 28.10. 1906
Michael b.1932
Renee b. 1937

Jack = Eileen
m. 1936
b. 8.12.1908
Dennis b.1937
Adrian b. 1938
Ann b. 1938
Peter b. 1942
Nora b 1942

David
b. 20.6.1911

Charlie
(1880 –1964)

=

Sarah
Ellen
Mines
(1880 – 1932)

Ruby = Tom
m. 1938
b. 29.11. 1913
Molly b.1943
Alan b. 1947

Connie = Fred
m. 1941
b. 5.8.1916
Rosemary b 1944

Pete = Sybil
m. 25.4.1942
b. 19.4.1920
Diana b.1944
Mary b.1945
(b.1955 Hilary)

Pauline = Reg
m. 1941
b. 19.4.1920
Geoffrey b.1943
(b.1954 Richard)

Audrey
b. 14.7.1928

24.1 Farmbrough family tree, Hazlemere Branch

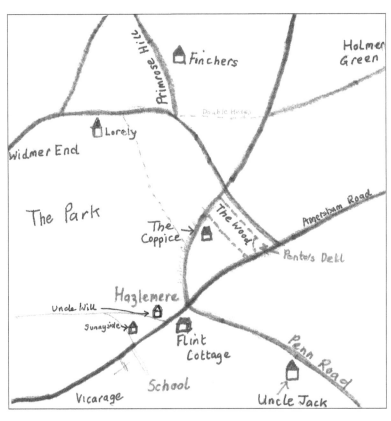

24.2 Map of Hazlemere showing Sunnyside, Uncle Will and Lorely

Renee's Story

Renee can just remember the first time she was evacuated to Buckinghamshire from London: it was during the Blitz in the Second World War. Renee was a quiet, placid little girl with blonde shoulder-length curly hair; she had a ready smile and was articulate for her age. Renee was only a toddler when she stayed with her Aunty Ruby, her mother's sister, whose home was called Lorely, a between the-wars bungalow at Widmer End.

Ruby was bright, cheerful, hardworking, and kind. Taking over from her sister Phyl in 1930, Ruby helped run the family home at The Coppice until she married her sweetheart Tom Barker, in December 1938, and they bought Lorely, at Brimmers Hill, Widmer End. To any visitor, Ruby's home was always welcoming, spick and span, and smelt of Pears toilet soap; Ruby was a great homemaker and life there was well ordered and happy.

A favourite with Renee was Ruby's friendly Welsh Border Collie, called Sally.

"When we've tidied the house, we'll walk Sally through The Park to see your grandfathers at Hazlemere," said Ruby.

"Can we visit Grampy Will and Grampy Charlie?" asked Renee.

Renee's brother, Michael, seven years older, was also evacuated, but he stayed with their paternal grandfather, Will, who lived in Green Street, Hazlemere, and Grampy Charlie lived at The Coppice on Holmer Green Road (Will and Charlie were brothers).

Even though the war was still going on, the Blitz eventually subsided and Michael and Renee returned home to live with their parents, Phyl and Reg, in North London. Renee started school, but, by 1944, another terrifying "doodlebug" bombing attack made a further evacuation necessary. This time she stayed with another of her mother's sisters, Marj.

Marj, born 1906, was small, bright, and sharp. She was the second daughter of Charlie and Sarah, and she married Bert Kilroy, a kindly man, in 1936. They lived in a semi-detached house in Hazlemere called "Sunnyside". Their first daughter, Heather, was born in 1939.

At the news of the doodlebugs, Marj spoke to Phyl on the 'phone:

"It makes sense for Renee to come and stay with Heather and me at Sunnyside," said Marj – Renee and Heather were close friends.

"Renee and Heather can go to school together, it's so handy living opposite."

To Renee, Hazlemere was full of birdsong and wildflowers, but at school she found she was repeating many of the lessons learned a year earlier in London. Her brother Michael, a few years ahead of her, was also at Hazlemere school, however, again, he was staying with their grandfather Will.

Renee liked to visit her grandfather Charlie at The Coppice; there was a special rapport between them, possibly because she was his first granddaughter, born five years after the death of his wife Sarah.

"Grampy Charlie, are there fairies in your garden?" asked Renee.

"Let's go and have a look," he would say, lifting petals and leaves as the two of them walked, hand in hand, round the garden.

Sometimes he would talk about her parents:

"I wonder what Reg the Fireman is doing today?" Renee's father had been assigned to work with the London Fire Brigade.

24.3 Renee and Michael at The Coppice with their aunt Audrey in the middle.

24.4 Phyl visits Michael and Renee at The Coppice during the 1944 evacuation *

After the war Renee continued to visit Hazlemere during school holidays, staying with Marj and family, but visiting us at Primrose Hill and her other cousins in the extended Farmbrough family at Hazlemere.

At Lorely, Ruby now had a family of her own; soon after her and Tom's marriage he was called up to the Army, and it was several years later that their daughter, Molly, was born in September 1943 and a son, Alan, arrived just after the end of the war. Tom returned to a perfect home and ideal family.

In late 1950 the 'phone lines to Phyl in Wood Green were busy because Ruby needed radical surgery for breast cancer. The tables were turned and this time Phyl was able to offer accommodation in London for Molly. During her stay Renee helped Molly settle into life in a large London house where everything was strange: they had an upstairs, in the street there were houses on both sides of the road, pavements, and

---

* *The body language in the above picture of Phyl's visit tells the anguish of separation and evacuation. For Phyl and Reg, two of their homes in London were "bombed out" and nothing was salvaged. In the picture, Michael looks fed up and resigned, and Renee looks unhappy and awkward, both aware that they were obliged to conform.*

streetlights. Molly played at home with Aunty Phyl during the day while her cousins, Michael and Renee, went to school.

"Don't worry about missing school, Molly," said Renee,

"I'll help you with your reading and writing; we'll do a bit every day, so you won't be left behind when you go home."

Renee was attending a dance class and took the opportunity to teach Molly some of the steps and routines.

"Four steps on the diagonal from the two armchairs to meet in the middle, and back again."

Molly was very like Renee in many ways: quiet, cheerful, considerate and she had strong blonde hair in two thick plaits.

Ruby made a good recovery and soon her children were back home with her. Glad to be back to normal, Ruby said to Tom:

"When Renee comes to Hazlemere in the summer, why don't we have a bit of a do in the garden?" Tom warmed to this idea and added:

"If I know Renee, when she hears about a party, she will want to put on some sort of performance, Molly is still talking about their dance routine."

The Garden Party

This story is about a family garden party, and how that event and the photograph taken at the time, has resonated within the family.

In 1951 while Renee was staying at Sunnyside with the Kilroy family for a summer holiday, preparations were underway for a garden party at Lorely, the home of her Aunty Ruby and Uncle Tom and our cousins, Molly and Alan. Renee was planning a performance set to music, by herself and three cousins, Heather, Molly and Margaret; and she had prepared a *programme of entertainments*. Rehearsals were held in the garden at Sunnyside using music from a wind-up HMV gramophone, and Aunty Marj found some old tea towels and curtains to augment the colourful crepe paper Renee had brought for the fancy-dress costumes.

The day of the party dawned sunny and warm, perfect for outside entertainment. At Sunnyside, Renee was looking for a suitable bag to hang on her bicycle handlebars:

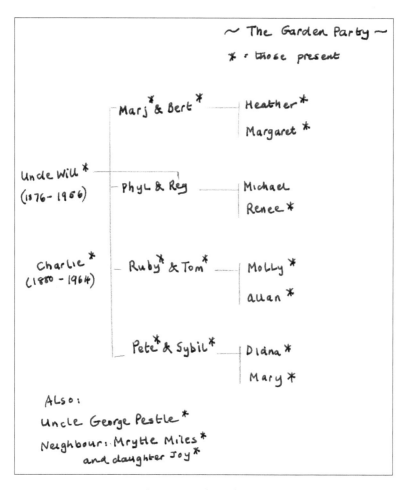

24.5 Guests at the garden party

24.6
Back row: George Pestle, Charlie Farmbrough, Renee Farmbrough,
Heather Kilroy, Bert Kilroy, Mrs Miles (neighbour), Tom Barker.
Middle row: Diana Farmbrough, Molly Barker, Ruby Barker,
Marj Kilroy, Sybil Farmbrough (with Mary on her lap).
Front row: Margaret Kilroy, Alan Barker, Joy Miles (neighbour's daughter).
Bottom LH corner: WF = William Farmbrough

"I want something big enough to pack our costumes for the tableau and dances," she said, and Heather added:

"Don't forget the gramophone record, we must be careful to put it between the costumes so it doesn't get damaged on the ride through The Park."

Renee and Heather set off for Lorely, followed a bit later by Bert and Marj with Margaret on the rear seat on her mother's bike.

Once they reached Lorely, Renee and Heather took their bikes to the back of the bungalow and used the French doors on the back terrace to go into the rear sitting room and change. It was then they found that disaster had struck; looking in the bag, Renee discovered that the record was in pieces. Hearing Renee and Heather's shrieks and wails from the sitting room; Tom rushed in to find out what was wrong.

"It's all ruined, we can't do the show without the music," Renee sobbed. Tom put his arm round her shoulder, "Dry your tears Renee, perhaps we can find another record."

"It won't be the same, we've rehearsed all our movements to that tune," said Heather.

Tom could see Renee and Heather were distraught, so he thought of something to console the two girls and told them:

"You're not the only ones upset today. This morning I went to buy a more powerful motorbike for my combination (*a motorbike and sidecar*) but the chap selling it told me he had changed his mind. So, I've got to keep looking."

Heather and Renee tried to look sympathetic, but his story didn't help their dilemma, and they were left wondering how they could perform without music.

At Finchers, Mary and I were looking forward to the party in our aunt and uncle's garden. We visited Lorely regularly, and eagerly anticipated waiting for their cuckoo clock in the hall to pop out and call the hour. At Lorely there were two other things we didn't own and particularly enjoyed – a piano, and Sally, their Welsh Border Collie.

We set off in the car from Primrose Hill, in good time for Dad to help Tom put the chairs out and Mum, with the fairy cakes she had made, to help Ruby with preparations for tea. On the way we overheard Mum and Dad talking in low voices:

"I was so scared when Ruby got cancer, so often it's a death sentence."

"I know how you feel about Ruby, how she brought you up and made a loving home for you. She made me welcome when I joined the family and I'm very fond of her too," Mum replied.

"Well, I'm glad the operation is over and Ruby's home with Tom and the children. She's looking so well; I can understand them wanting to have a party to celebrate."

On arrival we children went off as usual to find Alan and Joy in the garden, Mum took her cakes to the kitchen and found Ruby and her neighbour Myrtle.

Dad, hearing raised voices in the sitting room, went to find out what was up, and learning about the damaged record, immediately wanted to help, so he said:

"We can't have the afternoon spoilt over a broken gramophone record. I know – we've got a copy of that record at Finchers, I'll slip back home and fetch it." So, popping his head into the kitchen to tell Ruby and Sybil where he was going, he got in the car and drove back to Finchers.

More people were arriving: Grampy Farmbrough on his motorbike, with Uncle George Pestle on the pillion (Grampy always left his motorbike on its stand on the front path). Aunty Marj with Margaret, Uncle Bert and Uncle Will Farmbrough who had caught them up, all parked their bikes round the back; and Uncle Will Farmbrough went to the sitting room with his camera bag to check his camera settings, and that's when he heard about the broken record and Dad's solution to the problem.

With Mum, Marj and Ruby's neighbour, Myrtle Miles, each having brought cake tins lined with greaseproof paper and containing sandwiches or cakes, the excitement and laughter in the kitchen was mounting. Ruby took control:

"We'll put the sandwiches on these plates and cover them with a damp tea towel," she said and turning to Mum and Marj said:

"If we keep the cakes in their tins, we can pile them on top of each other to save space, until we're ready to eat."

"You must let us help you later, when the food's served," said Mum.

"No, thank you for your offer; I'm sure I shall manage with Heather and Renee. I want you, Marj and Myrtle to stay in the garden and enjoy the party." Ruby was adamant.

With the prospect of music again, all was not lost, so the cousins Renee, Heather, Molly and Margaret changed into their fancy-dress costumes while Bert helped Tom set out the tables and chairs facing the rose garden, close to the house. The garden was looking a picture in the afternoon sun, the trees and hedges were full of birdsong, and everyone admired Tom's colourful perfumed roses.

Uncle Will, who had unstrapped his tripod from the crossbar on his bike and set his camera on it, took the opportunity to assemble everyone for a group photograph but when everyone was satisfactorily assembled, he went ahead without Dad, who had yet to return with the recording, so he was missing from the picture.

Eventually when Dad reappeared with the replacement record, the entertainment got underway. The tableau of a princess (Renee) and maidens (Heather, Margaret and Molly) wandering through a forest changed into a dance sequence where each cousin, in turn, represented different countries, Molly was a little Dutch girl. The gramophone rang out with the notes of *Tales from Vienna Woods* and everyone sang along with the well-known tune. There was even an encore.

Later, Renee and Heather handed round plates of egg, fish paste and jam sandwiches; followed by fruit cake and individual fairy cakes and bowls of jelly. The adults drank tea and for the children there was Kia Ora Orange Squash. Afterwards, as the adults talked, we children played hide and seek and took turns on the garden swing – it seemed as though these long summer days would go on for ever.

What do I remember of that day? A wasp stung me on the mouth; it had been eating my cake, and I cried.

The remarkable photograph made on that day serves not only as a record of a happy event and of deeply treasured family relationships, but also as a reminder of how quickly lives can be changed for ever. In only a few short months, Ruby's cancer returned and by November she had died. The whole family were stunned and grieved deeply for the tragic loss of Ruby at such a young age.

In the immediate aftermath Molly returned to London to live with Phyl and family and Alan came to stay with us at Finchers. When their dad, Tom, was ready to have them home, he was supported by his mother, Nanny Barker, who walked most days from her home at Cosy Corner to help keep on top of the housework at Lorely.

The strain of loss caused Tom to develop a stomach ulcer, which in those days was treated with a nocturnal milk drip into his stomach. He later married Bett, the widow of a work colleague, amalgamating their two families. Even later, with Bett's brother and sister-in law, they bought and ran a dairy farm in Devon.

Molly made a successful marriage; she and her husband, Fred, had three children and they now enjoy being great grandparents.

Alan married Hazel and they live near Hazlemere.

Renee worked for the World Wildlife Fund in Geneva. She was happily married to Roger and they had two children; she still lives in Switzerland.

25

The Black Cat Stamp Album

Acquired by saving gift coupons from Craven A cigarette company, this Black Cat Stamp Album has entwined its many lives through the Farmbrough family for over a century. My Great Uncle Will Farmbrough presented it to his son Reginald at the end of the Great War. But Reginald's interest in stamps was short-lived, and before long the Black Cat was returned to his father, who then found another suitable recipient, and wrote to his nephew Pete (our dad) in the late 1920s:

25.1 Uncle Will's letter

Translation:

Dear Peter,

At last I am sending you the Stamp Album promised; you will see there are a few stamps in it already, to give you a start. These were mostly put in by Reg to whom I gave the Album some years ago, but he got tired of it & sold it to me back again as he wanted to buy something more exciting. I think he bought some silkworms, or perhaps it was marbles, anyhow altho' his name is in it, it is my property to give & is not stolen from his toy box under the bed! Hope you had a good time at the Scouts Wolfs (crossed out) cubs outing and did your good deed alright.

Your affect Uncle Will.

Uncle Will was an accomplished photographer and became a seafarer, working as a steward for the Union Castle Shipping Line. The Union Castle slogan was: *"Every Thursday at 4 o'clock a Union Castle Liner departs Southampton bound for Cape Town".*

In later life, when not at sea, he participated in Hazlemere village life, putting on magic lantern shows and entertainments. Uncle Will, universally remembered with affection, was a man of mystery, adventure, and tales of exotic places.

Pete (our dad) was still at school when he became the owner of the glamourous Black Cat Album. He was pleased to find it contained stamps from the reigns of Queen Victoria, Edward VII and George V, from all over the British Empire. Pete did his best to add to his collection, but having limited means to buy stamps, he had to wait for interesting stamps to arrive by post, and this inevitably slowed his progress.

By 1936 Pete had left school and was beginning his seven-year engineering apprenticeship; his interest in stamps had taken a back seat to his passion for motorbikes. However, that year presented an opportunity too good for any stamp collector to miss. The death of King George V in January, the abdication of his son (the uncrowned

Edward VIII), followed by the accession to the throne of King George VI in December, reignited Pete's enthusiasm. The Black Cat's wiles had worked their magic, and its *Great Britain and Ireland* pages were quickly adorned with bright new issues for Edward VIII and George VI.

To preserve its pristine condition and as a mark of Pete's pride of ownership, the Black Cat Album was stored at home in the Canterbury bookcase in the front room at The Coppice, away from the rough and tumble of family life.

And there it stayed for the next fifteen years.

Until, in the early 1950s, our dad introduced my sister Mary and me to the Black Cat Album. On our weekly visits to The Coppice, Dad would sometimes take us into the front room. Picking up his album, he held it open at the first page which read:

'British Empire, Great Britain and Ireland,
Stamps first issued 1840.
Great Britain the first country to issue Postage Stamps'.

Then he said:

"Look here at this page, 'British Empire, Asia – India. Stamps first issued 1854' – the first line is Queen Victoria, three pies, a half anna and a one anna*. The next line is Edward the Seventh, three pies, one anna, two annas, and that's how it goes on down the page, one line for each design."

Mary and I were impressed with the detail and knowledge needed to match a stamp to a country and then get it in the right place on the page:

"How do you know how much space to leave when you stick the stamps in?" we asked.

Dad laughed and told us:

"That's easy, you use stamp hinges so you can move the stamps when more or better stamps come your way."

---

*   *Anna was the currency formerly used in British India, equal to one sixteenth of a rupee. It was subdivided into twelve pies.*

In this way Mary and I became aware of the skill needed to collect stamps; we took one last look before dad closed the album and returned the Black Cat to the bookcase.

In 1953, anticipating the issue of commemorative stamps for the coronation of the new Queen Elizabeth II, Dad felt the time had come for the Black Cat Album to leave The Coppice and move in with us at Finchers.

Postage stamps were made in High Wycombe by Harrison & Sons, whose factory was next door to where Dad worked (at JKO Cutters). Interest was growing about the new stamps with our young Queen's head on them. In the Coronation Year Mary and I collected all we could and stuck them in the Black Cat Album and marked the spaces on the page for the missing denominations.

As time went by, we recognised that the Black Cat was showing its age. The world was changing, the British and German Empires no longer existed, and countries had changed names:

British Empire:
Bechuanaland (became Botswana)
Central Africa (became Nyasaland)
East Africa (became Kenya)

The Black Cat had served its purpose; it had lured Mary and me into the world of stamp collecting and before long we had albums of our own.

From an advertisement in *Girl* comic, we bought packets of stamps for sixpence each: we felt quite grown-up queueing at the post office to buy a one shilling postal order to cover the cost and eagerly awaited the arrival of the latest Trusty Packet.

Swapping stamps with friends at school was good fun.

"Have you got any swaps?"

I carried an envelope with my swaps in my satchel. If asked, I would usually reply:

"I like unusual stamps with birds or flowers on," and got excited when I heard:

"I've got some triangles."

Triangles always looked good on the stamp album page and

I wondered what I would have to give up to get one. Some of our school friends collected Special Issues or Commonwealth countries like Australia or Canada.

As we filled the pages of our stamp albums, we became familiar with strange names like "Suomi", "Helvetia" and "Magyar" and discovered they meant Finland, Switzerland, and Hungary. In the process, our imaginations were stretched to far flung locations.

What happened to our interest in stamp collecting?

Was I distracted by the move to a new house, new school, new friends or was it the new conservatory where I could keep more budgerigars and start a collection of cacti and succulents?

Perhaps it was Elvis Presley singing 'A Fool Such As I', Buddy Holly with 'It Doesn't Matter Anymore', and Paul Anka singing 'Put Your Head on My Shoulder', all seductively crooning on Radio Luxemburg; that undermined my stamp collecting?

Is it possible that the unintended consequences of stamp collecting had more long-lasting and far-reaching effects?

Mary maintained her stamp collection and married a stamp collector. She and John lived and worked in Zambia (formerly Northern Rhodesia) for several years, and together they travelled the world extensively on holiday.

I developed an interest in natural history, botany and ornithology and visited over fifty countries, photographing people and wildlife; and I felt the irresistible need to record these trips with journals and albums.

A vestige of my stamp collecting days has remained: The Black Cat Album, now a hundred years old, and much the worse for wear, has uncurled from a long sleep and is enjoying yet another brief life.

26

Joseph Monk Farmbrough of Dinton

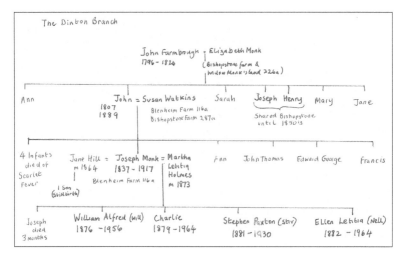

26.1 Farmbrough family tree, part of the Dinton Branch

In the kitchen at The Coppice, our grandfather's home, there was a stuffed badger's head with a riding crop looped round its neck, its beady eyes and glinting teeth grimacing at the whole room from a position high on the picture rail.

We children were fascinated with the badger and our grandfather would pick one of us up so that we could reach the snout, and say:

"Why don't you give Laughing Boy a stroke?"

We were intrigued and frightened at the same time. Sometimes he would take down the riding crop and twirl the leather thong in his hand and regale us with stories from long ago:

"We are going back about a hundred years: this crop belonged to my father, your great grandfather, Joseph Monk Farmbrough; he was a renowned horseman and would never be without his riding crop." (Hilary now has his riding crop in her sitting room.)

"In his younger days he was a hunting farmer; most farmers followed the hounds and rode over each other's fields: steeplechasing was the national sport. It was said that his horse was so large it could clear any hedge or ditch in the area; and that when he rode home late from business in Aylesbury, his horse would clear the Dinton Turnpike – and the toll keeper, recognising the sound of the hooves, stayed indoors."

"Why was he called Joseph Monk?" we asked.

Grampy settled into his armchair and said:

"He already had an Uncle Joseph, and Monk – his second name – was after his grandmother Elizabeth Monk; it helped tell the two Josephs apart."

We moved round the table to be nearer Grampy, our curiosity aroused, we wanted to know more, and asked:

"Where did he live?"

Grampy slowly lit his pipe, and after a good pull, said:

"Well, his story begins at Dinton to the west of Aylesbury, he was born in 1837 at Blenheim Farm (that's the same farm where I was born); his uncles, Joseph and Henry, were at Bishopstone farm, in the next village. Together the two farms made a sizeable holding and created work for a lot of farm labourers."

Gradually, we came to know more of Joseph Monk's story. On Sunday afternoons, after our dad bought his first car in 1949, our grandfather sometimes joined us for a ride out. One sunny spring day we went to Dinton, and leaving the car, our grandfather made for the church. Walking up through the churchyard towards the south door, he stopped and rubbed the lichen away from the inscription on two headstones:

"These are the graves of my grandparents, Joseph Monk's parents, John and Susan (Watkins) Farmbrough."

He then went on to tell us that they lost their first three sons to scarlet fever, and when Joseph Monk was born, in 1837, he was their

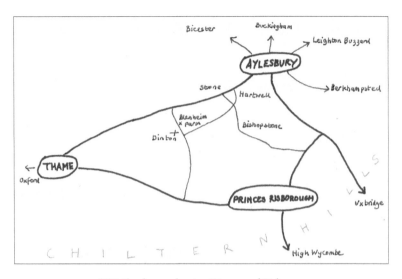

26.2 Sketch map showing Dinton and Bishopstone

first child to survive. His parents doted on him because he was their longed-for son and heir. The family were making a good living from farming during the 1840s and it was probably the thing to do, so Joseph Monk was sent to Thame Grammar School where, amongst other things, he learnt the manners of a gentleman and to speak French. The family were expecting Joseph Monk to take over both farms, Dinton and Bishopstone, and possibly a third farm.

Our grandfather said:

"I remember him reading from his French pocket testament – until the end of his life. There was a tale in the family that my father made influential friends and, as the result of a wager with one of the Rothschilds, every year without fail, a licence for his dog arrived in the post."

Dinton was only a small village, and we were looking out from the churchyard across open fields, towards the Chiltern Hills, so we wanted to know:

"Where's the farm where you were born?"

We walked up the road to the north of the church and after a short distance, on the opposite side, came to a thatched house sideways on to the road.

26.3 Blenheim Farmhouse, 1910

"This is Blenheim Farm where Joseph Monk was born. He worked alongside his father, John, until the tenancy at Bishopstone became vacant in the 1850s, and then his father ran both farms until Joseph Monk took over Blenheim on his own."

There were parts of the story our grandfather didn't tell us. From later research we found out that Joseph Monk grew into his role as a gentleman farmer. There are press reports of him playing an active part in village life, as churchwarden, village constable, and being a signatory to a petition for improvements to the village school.

In 1864, at the age of 27, he married Jane Hill and they had a son who died at birth; Jane survived, but no more children were born and she too died a few years later.

An extract from *The Bucks Herald* dated 15 February 1873, reported the outcome of an inquest into a fatal traffic accident that involved Joseph Monk and two friends on the Hartwell Road. The inquest was heard at the Harrow Inn, close to the scene of the accident. Both vehicles were on their way home from Aylesbury market on Saturday afternoon, 25 January 1873.

William Slade, the son of the victim, said they were coming home with his donkey cart; his father riding and he was walking alongside. He stopped to speak to a friend, and his father alighted from the cart and led the donkey to the far side of the road about 300 yards ahead. Mr Farmbrough, a farmer from Dinton, came along with his horse and spring cart and two other people, one of whom was driving. Although it was 25 January, the night was not very dark, but the spring cart was driving at a fair pace, about nine miles an hour; they drove past his father and knocked him down. He didn't think his father was badly injured, but he died ten days later.

Even though the inquest jury agreed "Accidental Death", such an incident would undoubtedly have created a stir in a close-knit community.

Not long after the accident, in August of the same year, Joseph Monk (now 35 years old) married again, his new wife was Martha Letitia Holmes (our great grandmother); but again, the firstborn son died the following September. Then, at last, two more boys were born, William in 1876 (Uncle Will) and Charlie in 1879 (our grandfather).

Later that year we again drove to Dinton, it was a mellow autumn day. We parked just below the church beside the village stocks on a triangle of grass. Our grandfather showed us where he used to find walnuts fallen from the tree there. We walked up to Blenheim Farm and, looking at the farmhouse, our grandfather (Charlie) continued the story:

"They say that on the day I was born, my father planted a pear tree on the gable end wall and look, it's still there, bearing fruit: isn't that remarkable?"

We agreed with him and felt it unfair that they were not his pears:

"Why don't our family still live here at Blenheim Farm?"

Grampy lowered his voice and continued:

"It was the start of four years of bad harvests and poor prices for corn." Previously poor harvests and scarce supplies meant higher prices to compensate, but cheap grain coming from America undercut the price.

"My father bought a flock of sheep from a local farmer called Ing, he was a friend of the family, and my father was hoping to make a return on them. They all died of liver fluke and it was a loss he could ill afford. After that my father often said, 'Never trust an Ing'."

Our grandfather went on to explain that the decline in agriculture started with the Enclosure Acts when farm-labouring families were driven off the land to find industrial work. His father recognised that times were hard and it was difficult to see a future for his young family. He decided rather than borrow money and run into debt, he would make an arrangement with his creditors. An advertisement was published in *The Bucks Herald* on Saturday 27 December 1879, by order of the Registrar of the Buckinghamshire County Court, appointing a trustee in bankruptcy. This public notice rendered Joseph Monk bankrupt. He was forty-two years old.

On the 1881 census, the family were still living at Dinton. Joseph Monk was working as a rate collector. A third son, Stephen Paxton (known as Uncle Stiv), was born that year and a daughter, Ellen Letitia (known as Aunt Nell), in 1882.

Eventually, affairs at Dinton were settled and, finding work as a farm bailiff at Abridge, the family moved to Essex. However, farmers everywhere were struggling. This period became known as *the Great Agricultural Depression* and farming didn't properly recover until after the Second World War. The family moved to Woodford and Joseph Monk found clerical work.

Back at The Coppice, sitting round the kitchen table one Sunday teatime, we were drinking tea, Grampy cutting bread and jam, still wearing his cap. Seated at the table and with bread on his plate, he carried on with his story, saying:

"Growing up in Essex away from our roots meant we were a close-knit family. We had good schooling and we moved with the times."

Mary and I found it hard to imagine our grandfather as a young man, but we could see our parents nodding and listening intently to Grampy's tale – it clearly matched their approach to life.

Grampy pointed towards the sideboard and added:

26.4 Joseph Mony Farmbrough and Family:
Standing: Stephen Paxton (Stiv), Charlie, William Alfred (Will)
Seated: Joseph Monk, Martha Letitia, Ellen Letitia (Nell)

"Those wine decanters are from the time I was working as a clerk with a wine merchant: I liked the work but the pay was poor. About the time Queen Victoria died, I met and courted Sarah Ellen Mines (your grandmother), soon after that we moved back to Bucks, I was in my twenties and found better-paid work in the furniture industry."

Mum was looking approvingly at the two glass decanters on either end of the mahogany sideboard – they had wide bases and fluted sides that splayed out for the glass stoppers at the top. Mary and I had never seen any wine in them, but we knew from overhearing conversations, that Grampy's favourite wine was something called "White Graves".

Grampy was back in his armchair, and had lit his pipe:

"One way and another, my brothers and sister made their living away from farming. Will became a ship's steward on the Union Castle line. Stiv was a signalman on the Great Eastern Railway, and Nell was a schoolteacher before she married."

Grampy puffed on his pipe with a satisfied look, having told us about his life before he came to Hazlemere. To Mary and I, it all seemed so long ago; we knew Uncle Will, who lived in Green Street, just up the road in Hazlemere; and we knew of Aunt Nell, who married a Great Eastern Signalman at Marks Tey in Essex and she was landlady of The Railway Tavern there, because Grampy went to stay with her for a week every summer. We didn't know Uncle Stiv, who had died in 1930, but we had heard Dad talking about his daughter, his cousin Millie.

Our grandmother, Martha Letitia Holmes, died soon after Nell's wedding in 1910, and after that Joseph Monk became a regular visitor at Flint Cottage and enjoyed spending time with his (then) four grandchildren: Winifred who was eight when her grandmother died, Marjorie two years younger, Phyl only four, and Jack still a toddler. With the turning of the years and the arrival of more grandchildren, each was greeted warmly by Joseph Monk, their "Gramp Farmbrough". David was born in 1911, Ruby came next in 1913 and baby Connie arrived in 1916. These older children later recalled some of his tales:

When Joseph Monk was still at Blenheim Farm, one of the farm labourers, knowing how his employer liked riddles, asked him:

"Mr. Farmbrough, can you tell me whether a thing is lost if you know where it is?"

And Joseph Monk replied in a matter-of-fact way:

"Of course, it can't be lost if you know where it is."

Encouraged by this reply, the labourer continued:

"Well, your axe is in the bottom of the pond; I didn't put it there on purpose, it just flew out of me 'and."

On another occasion Joseph Monk told his grandchildren about a panic at Blenheim Farm when he was a young lad and one of the farm cats jumped into the fire and ran up the chimney, and his father was summoned:

"Fader, Fader, come quickly, the black-faced piveney has gone to the high top of the mountain; if you don't soon fetch the ablution, we shall all be ockaloram."

Which apparently translates to:

"Father, Father, come quickly, the black cat has gone up the chimney; there will be trouble if you don't fetch some water."

When living at Dinton, Joseph Monk never missed a market day at Aylesbury. At one time he kept so large a horse that the landlord of the inn where he put up on market day made a concession and fitted a special wide stall for it.

Towards the end of his life when Joseph Monk was living in Hazlemere, our Uncle David, still a schoolboy, came home very pleased with himself, with two ducks, one under each arm; he had caught them on the pond in Post Office Lane next to Hazlemere School. Being an upright citizen and model grandfather, Joseph Monk made him return them, saying they were not his to take.

These tales have become woven into the myths and legends of the Farmbrough family and still make family members chuckle today.

Our grandfather leaned forward in his armchair and tapped out his pipe on the side of the fireplace; speaking softly he said,

"I was with my father on 22 December 1917 when he died; it was thirty-eight years after he was made bankrupt at Dinton, and seven years after our mother died. He was eighty years old. It was the end of an era."

26.5 Joseph Monk Farmbrough in about 1900 taken by Will Farmbrough, his son.

27

The Farmbrough Connection

As we were growing up, we were aware that those with the family name "Farmbrough" were from a large, old, Bucks family. Various strands of research had been recorded in "The Red Book", showing part of the family tree from 1777 – 1854, and extracts from the Hartwell Archive giving charters and manorial records referring to the Farmbrough family from 1290 – 1776. A branch of Farmbroughs connected with the Rose family had been researched, and a William J Farmbrough of New York produced a two-hundred-year tree of a group that became known as the Harrow Branch.

In 1976 the Rev. J.L. McLelland Farmbrough wrote to all the Farmbroughs in the telephone directory, enlisting their help and, with the discovery of missing links, over the following four years it became possible to complete his research and eventually to connect all the living Farmbroughs, in various branches, to a family tree that goes back to the thirteenth century.

During the research period, an occasional newsletter was produced for those family members who were interested, and on completion of the project, there was considerable demand for a meeting and exposition.

At the first Family Gathering in 1977, the Family Tree was unveiled: it measures nearly 10 feet by 3 feet and contains over a thousand names. From it, all living Farmbroughs can trace their ancestry back to one man, Peter Farmbrough (*signed Peter de Famboro in documents in the Bodleian Library in Oxford),* who lived at Hartwell in 1270. Like his descendants, he was a freeman, a yeoman farmer, tilling the land in the Vale of Aylesbury and although younger sons left the land, his heirs continued for the next eighteen generations until Joseph Monk, the last Farmbrough at Blenheim Farm at Dinton, rather than face financial ruin and hardship, gave up his farm and eventually the farming way of life.

27.1 The team who completed the work of
Rev. J.L. McLelland Farmbrough, leaning over the family tree:
Terry Farmbrough, Michael Farmbrough and David O'Neale.

In the above picture Terry Farmbrough is holding a copy of his book, A History of the Farmbrough Family 1250 – 1900. His introduction summarises the seven-hundred-year history of the Farmbrough family – a vast pageant of independently minded yeoman farmers – in which throughout, we find no connection to royalty, or great wealth. To most family history researchers this would be a disappointment, but Terry reminds us of a passage from *Robinson Crusoe* which suggests that the best state in the world most suited to human happiness is the upper station of low life, free of miseries and hardships and sufferings of labour, but not embarrassed with the pride, luxury, ambition and envy of the upper part of mankind.

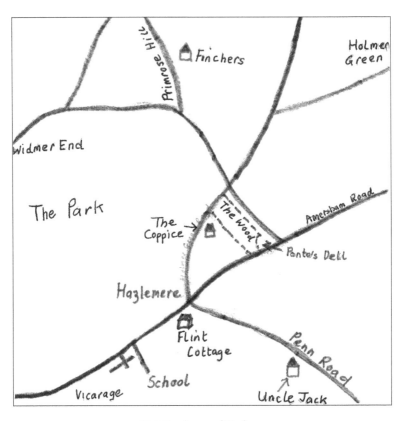

28.1 Sketch map of Hazlemere

28

Uncle David – Countryman, Sailor, Poacher, and Conservationist

This is the story of Uncle David and of The Coppice, my grandfather's house. Except for his war service, David lived in the same house for over seventy years: from the time it was built in the mid-1920s, until it was demolished towards the end of the century.

David George Farmbrough was born on 20 June 1911, the fifth child of Charlie and Sarah Ellen Farmbrough who, at that time, lived at Flint Cottage, Hazlemere Crossroads. His four siblings were all born in the previous nine years: Winifred (Win), Marjorie (Marj), Phillis (Phyl) and John Charles Fyfield (known as Jack). David is on the right of the family photograph (Image 06.02) taken at the birth of the Farmbrough twins in April 1920.

In turn, the children attended Hazlemere Church of England School, and the boys sang in the church choir with their father, Charlie. The girls sang in the school choir.

Between the two world wars the population of High Wycombe grew, as people moved to the area to look for work and the pressure on housing increased. My grandfather had a steady job in the furniture industry and in the 1920s he bought a piece of land on Holmer Green Road at Hazlemere and built a bungalow for his growing family; they called it The Coppice. It was beside a wood.

By the time the family moved, there were nine children: after David came Ruby, Miriam (known as Connie), and twins Pauline and Peter (our dad). A tenth child, Audrey, was born in 1928.

Having left school at the age of fourteen, the two older girls, Win and Marj, had been living and working in service since before the First World War.

At the new bungalow there was a smart leaded stove in the kitchen, which was the hub of the home, giving direct access to three bedrooms, a sitting room and a lobby leading to the pantry, scullery, and bathroom. Rainwater was collected in a well and hand pumped to the sink in the scullery. A copper boiler in the bathroom heated water for washing and bathing.

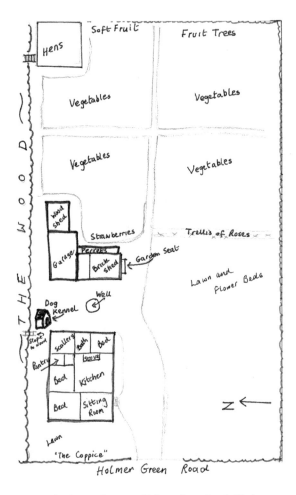

28.2 The Coppice layout at Holmer Green Road, Hazlemere

28.3 The Farmbroughs at The Coppice, 1926
Back from left: Will, Charlie, Arthur Spicer, Jack, dog Toby.
Middle from left: Win, Sarah Ellen, Connie, George Pestle, Ruby, Reg (son of Will) Phyl,
Front: Peter, Pauline, (not present Marj or David)

In 1924 David left school and took a job at The Park, at Hazlemere, owned by a Marlow brewing family called Leadbetter. It was conveniently located, just across the road from The Coppice. Workers were needed on the farm, and to help with the Leadbetter's menagerie of exotic animals (including lions, camels, and a jackal, in all there were over sixty animals, including carthorses). David was good with animals, it was work he loved and he probably would have continued at The Park, but when war broke out in 1939, he joined the Navy.

28.4 David in naval uniform

My first recollection of David was when he came home from the Navy. By then he was in his mid-thirties, a small slight figure with short dark hair. He was slow of speech and good-natured and he had a ready, lopsided smile. One side of his face was affected by Bell's palsy and his left eye had a squint – we children found this fascinating. He usually wore plimsolls, drill trousers and an open-necked shirt, but when the occasion demanded, he cleaned up well and wore a sports jacket, flannel trousers, leather shoes and a necktie.

As an uncle he always had time for us children and was ready with a riddle or tongue-twister to entertain us:

Q. Why did the owl howl?
A. Because the woodpecker would peck her.

Peter Piper picked a peck of pickled peppers. A peck of pickled peppers Peter Piper picked. If Peter Piper picked a peck of pickled peppers, where's the peck of pickled peppers Peter Piper picked?

Newly demobilised and looking for a job, he moved back into The Coppice, with our grandfather, and at that time Pauline, her husband Reg and their son, our cousin Geoffrey, were there as well. Scamp,

a Welsh Border Collie, rescued after a Canadian airman abandoned him at the end of the war, lived in the kennel outside the back door. He was a friendly dog and dearly loved.

Pauline, Reg and Geoffrey moved out of The Coppice to their own home at Holmer Green in 1950, leaving Grampy, David and Scamp to manage on their own.

A countryman, David liked to read about the countryside as

28.5 Geoffrey and Scamp at The Coppice

well as roam the fields and hedgerows. On a side table in the kitchen, along with The *Radio Times*, he kept a current copy of *The Field* magazine. His favourite author was Samuel Pepys, and he would refer to facts and scenes from the famous diaries and Mum, knowing there were several volumes, would ask him:

"How're you getting on with Pepys?"

"Well, as Chief Secretary to the Admiralty 'e's been to the Forest of Dean to buy timber for new ships."

"That must have been an interesting job," said Mum.

"But 'e's also found out that the king's being cheated by 'cutting off square' – that's when the timber's measured on the short length and charged on the long length – and 'e says 'e's going to 'take pleasure' in correcting this."

"So, he had some scruples after all then?" asked Mum.

"If yer don't count 'is private life, tha' was a bit colourful!" joked David.

David's time in the Navy left a lasting impression on him and maybe that's when he discovered his love of poetry. His conversation was frequently interspersed with lines such as *"I must go down to the seas again, to the lonely sea and the sky"* from *Sea Fever* by John Masefield.

It was a family legend that when David returned from the Navy, he took out one of his shotguns and went for a walk. He came home with a hare, and announced: *"Home is the sailor, home from sea, And the hunter home from the hill."* A quote from Robert Louis Stevenson, *Requiem*.

David kept two shotguns by the chimney alcove in the kitchen and boxes of cartridges in the dresser drawer. He claimed to have once shot twenty wood pigeons with one cartridge.

At The Coppice, the brick shed faced into the backyard and was kept locked. An occasional peek into the dark interior revealed any game that needed hanging: rabbit, pigeon, hare, pheasant, or partridge.

The garage also faced into the backyard. It smelt of oil and metal tools, and housed David's motorbike and Grampy's Vespa. Mary and I spotted something strange:

"What's all these grey furry things hanging up?"

David replied:

"They be squirrel tails. There's a bounty on these 'ere tails. If I collect 'em up and take 'em to the police station, I can get a bob* each for 'em."

Mary and I were impressed,

"We only get sixpence a week pocket money."

"That there Forestry Commission, they wants rid of the greys, they be driving out the reds," he explained.

He kept ferrets, one albino male and two brown females housed in acrid-smelling hutches behind the brick shed. They were fed on bread and milk and they drank water. He claimed this made them keen for blood. He took them "rabbiting" on a farm at Bledlow Ridge, helping the farmer there to control the "vermin".

At the time, on our regular weekly visits, it all seemed perfectly normal to us that David kept dead animals in the brick shed, had ferrets lying in wait in their hutches to bite our inquisitive fingers and collected squirrel tails in the garage.

The woodshed was behind the garage and faced into the back garden; it was used for woodturning and was the domain of Uncle Jack, Grampy's eldest son, who lived at Penn Road with his wife and five children. As the door opened, a sharp smell of resin filled the air; inside, on the left, was a lathe on a bench in front of the south-facing window. The shelves to the side and rear were crammed with pieces of wood, some shaped and some still in blocks. The floor was thick with sawdust and shavings, and soft to walk on. Like our dad, Uncle Jack had served an apprenticeship as a precision engineer, but his heart was in wood turning. His skill was appreciated and in demand; he made items to order and was kept busy in his spare time. Jack turned an oak standard lamp for Mum and Dad's wedding in 1942; it lasted their entire marriage and has been inherited by their grandson, Adam.

There was a popular science fiction series on the wireless during the 1950s called *Journey Into Space*, and Grampy Farmbrough, Uncle David and Scamp regularly listened in and followed the stories. Later,

---

* *A 'bob' was salng for a shilling, and sixpence was a half shilling. In 2022 a shilling was worth 5p and a sixpence 2.5p.*

David would take Scamp for his regular evening walk through The Park to The Royal Standard public house at Widmer End; it was one of those pubs where there was an inner lobby with doors opening to the tap room on one side and the lounge on the other.

On arrival, David would signal to Scamp to wait in the lobby while he went in and ordered his drink. This would inevitably give rise to the question:

"Where's young Scamp this evenin'?"

To which David would reply:

"'e's been listening to that programme *Journey Into Space* and 'e's waitin' in the decompression chamber."

And then, as the next customer entered, David would click his fingers, and Scamp would follow, sauntering into the bar and wagging his tail.

During the years that Grampy and David were living on their own at The Coppice, at one time they thought to get a 'new-fangled' pressure cooker which, it was claimed, would save cooking time and fuel. Not long after the pressure cooker made an appearance, Grampy came home one evening to find a note from David: "I've had my dinner, yours is on the ceiling." This cautionary tale soon spread through the family.

After the war David worked at the Timber Research (TRADA) near Princes Risborough. He brought home off-cuts from the samples sent for testing. From these samples David liked to challenge Mary and me:

"You two ought to be able to recognise all the common British species of wood by the grain, what do you think this 'ere is?"

"It's got the same pattern as our school desks."

"Yes, tha's right, it's beech, it comes from beechy Bucks."

We learnt to recognise oak, birch, ash, elm, and walnut.

Another time David said:

"At the Timber Research, we gets samples from all over the world, this 'ere is mahogany, and smell this one, it's teak."

Mary and I turned them in our hands and smelt them,

"Aren't they lovely, dark and mysterious?"

They both had a distinct deep odour and texture.

We gradually became familiar with cedar, spruce, Bird's-eye-maple, sapele, iroko and muhuhu. This last sample was difficult to distinguish, and if in doubt we would say:

"It's muhuhu!" – and David would laugh.

On the north side of The Coppice was the wood. It stretched from Holmer Green Road to Ponto's Dell on Amersham Road, the area covered by the wood was probably little more than ten acres, and contained mainly beech trees. The wood was bounded on all sides with thick hedges to deter trespassers. For over sixty years the Farmbrough hens (some of whom were rescued from battery farms) spent their days in this wood, scratching about in natural surroundings, only returning to their fox-proof hen house to roost or lay eggs.

We children found an unfenced slope down into the wood beside the dog kennel, where we could stray and explore. We discovered dells where flint and chalk had been extracted in the past, now filled with deep layers of leaves, gently rotting away. Following narrow animal paths, we came across clearings with brambles and silver birch and we sometimes caught a glimpse of long-tailed tits or goldfinches as they flitted between the lower branches. On still days the whole wood had a cathedral-like feel, cool and still, the only sound being the wind rustling in the topmost branches.

28.6 Oil painting of David

David remained a bachelor all his life. He shared an interest in the natural world with his friend Norman King, a talented amateur wildlife artist who lived with his wife Nan at Holmer Green. The highlight of David's year was their annual camping holiday. On the Solway Firth they witnessed the spectacle of the autumn migration when large flocks of Barnacle geese from Svalbard, and other species that nest in the Arctic, gathered each winter.

Grampy died in 1964 and David lived on at The Coppice alone for another thirty years. After Norman died, David became an obsessive hoarder and recluse, his guns and motorbike were disposed of. Eventually our parents helped him find and move to a small flat at Hazlemere Crossroads. The Coppice was sold and demolished, making way for two new houses.

A smoker all his life, he didn't consult a doctor until near the end. He lived to be 89 years old and died in May 2000.

The wood is still there.

29

Let's Bury a Time Capsule!

The early 1950s ushered in a period of change. By this time my sister Mary and I were pupils at Hazlemere C of E School. At Finchers a washing machine, a vacuum cleaner, and a television set had appeared in the house and these made life both easier and more interesting.

Not all our relations were as keen to move with the times; Mum told us one of our aunts had said:

"I wouldn't use one of those vacuum cleaners, they suck up all the pile from your carpet, you won't have a carpet left by the end of the year."

Dad had changed to a better job at the home appliance company, Hoover. The routine of work, school, housework, house maintenance and gardening and going to church were now interspersed with trips out in the car: this was by far the most dynamic catalyst for change in our lives, and from its windows my sister and I were afforded a glimpse of life beyond Primrose Hill and our Hazlemere circle.

Nationally, the new Labour Government, elected in 1945, was making big changes to education and in the provision of a health service, and the country was slowly recovering from the Second World War. The Government instigated a Festival of Britain in 1951 to boost national morale; it was to be a showcase for the knowledge and skills of the British people and intended to set new standards for design and architecture. The main site was on the South Bank of the Thames in London, but there were touring exhibitions as well on land and sea which reached many locations as far away as Belfast and Glasgow.

Over half of the forty-nine million population of Britain participated in the exhibition one way or another.

Dad, ever the optimist, could see a brighter future for his country and his family and was keen to be part of the brave new world.

"Let's go to The South Bank Exhibition; we could park near Waterloo, and go round the Dome of Discovery and the Skylon," said Dad.

"I've seen some lovely fabrics by Lucienne Day in *Women's Weekly*; we could look out for them and even see 'contemporary' chairs made by her husband, Robin," enthused Mum.

In May 1951 King George VI and Queen Elizabeth attended the official opening of the Royal Festival Hall. The gala concert was conducted by two of Britain's most famous conductors, Sir Malcolm Sargent and Sir Adrian Boult. The journalist Bernard Levin said his first impression was as if he had been transported far into the future.

The festival closed in September 1951 and a month later a new Conservative government was elected. One of the first acts of the incoming Prime Minister Winston Churchill was to order clearance of the festival site on the grounds that it was a piece of socialist propaganda. Despite this clearance, an important legacy remained: it established a place for culture and the arts that eventually became home to not only the Royal Festival Hall, but also the National Film Theatre, Queen Elizabeth Hall, the Purcell Room and the National Theatre. (Today this Hall is the only remaining vestige of the Festival of Britain.)

Dad, along with thousands of returning servicemen, viewed the change of government with horror. The wilful attempts to discredit the Festival of Britain and proposals to dismantle the welfare state (on the grounds of expense) seemed like a betrayal of the ideals they had fought so long and hard for during the war. Dad feared the "brave new world" was slipping away.

Very shortly afterwards, in February 1952, King George VI died at Sandringham House in Norfolk, triggering a period of national mourning that was gradually lifted in June the following year, with the coronation of the twenty-six-year-old Queen Elizabeth II.

Just after the king's funeral, no one was surprised when Dad suggested:

"On Sunday let's drive over to Windsor; we can park down by the river, walk up by the railway station and we'll follow the route of the gun carriage that took the king's body to St. George's Chapel at the Castle."

"It would be good for the girls to remember this important time," Mum agreed.

Something similar happened in the summer of 1953, after watching the coronation on our new nine-inch screen television and to which our neighbours were also invited: a day trip to London would allow us to follow the route of the Gold State Coach down The Mall. We could marvel at the coronation banners and decorations and visit Westminster Abbey. It made a big impression, and Mary and I told our friends about it for weeks afterwards.

The following is a story that might have occurred if our parents had come from a different background, if there was money to spare. Life had taught our parents not to trust prosperity, and so the following scene is entirely imaginary:

One Saturday dinner time (our mid-day meal), Mum had cooked stuffed braised hearts with mashed potatoes, carrots, cabbage and gravy. As usual we ate in the kitchen, Mum and Dad sat side by side on the long side of the table looking out the window, Mary and I were squashed in on the other side. Dad said,

"Do you remember when we went to the Festival of Britain Exhibition, and walked round the outside of the Royal Festival Hall?"

"Yes, that was the building with all the big glass windows," I remembered.

"That's right. Well, I believe that a time capsule was buried under the foundation stone when they started construction in 1949. It was such a turning point after the war, I am glad it was marked in this way."

"What's a time capsule?" asked Mary.

"The idea is that when the building is demolished and the time capsule dug up, the things inside will tell people what it was like all that time ago when it was buried – a bit like lost treasure, but just everyday belongings," explained Dad, "and I wondered if we made a time capsule about our life today, what would we put in?"

Mum began to warm to the idea:

"I suppose it's no use putting things in that will rot or dissolve over time, so what about a set of 1950's coins? We could start with a farthing, halfpenny, penny, threepenny bit, sixpence, a shilling, a two-shilling piece and up to a half-crown."

Dad laughed:

"That's an improvement on my first idea, I thought a set of collar studs, because I wear collar-attached shirts nowadays, and someone in the future would scratch their heads wondering what they were for!"

Mum looked wistful:

"A Biro pen would be a good idea, to demonstrate progress from those old leaky fountain pens. But my Biro pen is very precious because Dad asked Aunty Ruby to buy this pen for me while he was in the military hospital and we could only exchange letters, it would be hard to let it go."

After thinking a while, Mary said:

"I am sure children in the future would be glad to know the games we played, like hopscotch, skipping, marbles, five stones and jacks. We could put a set of jacks and a bouncy ball in the time capsule."

I joined in and suggested:

"One thing that might puzzle children is French knitting. We could include a cotton reel with four pins, a short piece of knitting and a pin to knit with, but they might not know how to do it without instructions."

Mary had another idea:

"What about some transfers – you know those we soak in a saucer of water and peel off on the back of our hands. I like the Micky Mouse ones best."

By the time we had rounded off our dinner with stewed plums and custard, we had all contributed a suggestion, and in addition, and despite the possibility of loss from damp, we agreed we should include a photo of ourselves as a family.

After dinner, Dad went off to the garage to work on the car, while

Mary and I helped Mum with the washing-up and putting away. We used Omo soap powder in the washing-up water and considered ourselves very advanced because some people still used household soap, which left a terrible scum. We were talking about what people in the future would find interesting about us and Mary had the great idea of putting one of our coronation crowns in the capsule.

Mum reminded us:

"We've collected a lot of coronation souvenirs this year girls – plates, playing cards, biscuit tins, teaspoons and not forgetting the postage stamps."

I remembered:

"We've both got two coronation mugs, I could spare the one with the queen's head on, I want to keep the one with the queen on her horse."

Mary grinned and said:

"And best of all, the coronation brought us the television set!"

"Coronation mania!" laughed mum.

Later, Mum called:

"Tea's ready."

The kitchen table was set with a colourful tablecloth, our willow pattern plates, cups and saucers, the butter dish, a pot of raspberry jam and a plate of fairy cakes; a loaf of bread and the bread knife were on the breadboard. The kettle had been boiling on the stove and taking down the tea caddy from the mantelpiece, Mum put three spoons of tea leaves into the aluminium teapot, filled the pot with water, replaced the lid to let it brew.

"Look what I've come up with," said Dad.

"This old metal toolbox has a hasp and padlock; it would make an ideal time capsule. We could put our photograph and other things that might deteriorate in a quart milk bottle. If we seal the top with a cork and sealing wax, it should keep out the damp. The bottle should just fit inside the toolbox."

Mum chimed in, practical as ever,

"Let's finish our tea and then get a few things together and see if they will fit the time capsule."

Mary and I had been wondering:

"Where will we bury it, and will it be a secret?"

Dad had the answer:

"That's why I think you should let me bury it where I think best, and I shall be the only one to know."

After tea Mum went through her purse and Mary and I emptied our money boxes to find a complete set of coins, and as we collected the items for our time capsule Mary found her coronation crown, and I my coronation mug

But of course, this didn't really happen. Our parents would never consider burying eleven shillings and fourpence three farthings.* The last thing they wanted was to encourage profligacy in their daughters. It was important to them that we girls grew up with a respect for money and to take care when spending it.

---

* *(The total value of a set of coins in old money worth about £19 in 2022 – source CPI Inflation Calculator) The average weekly wage for men in 1953 was just over £9, and for women £5.*

30

Everyone Sang

It seemed that during those years at Finchers we were surrounded by music and song. At home the wireless was tuned to the Light Programme which had a good selection of music programmes and was on all day from when Dad got up in the morning; Mum sang along with the wireless as she did her housework in the mornings, and then after we children were in bed Mum and Dad would tune into a music programme on the Home Service.

Sometimes they would get out their wind-up HMV gramophone and play records of songs by Turner Layton such as: *After You've Gone*, *Pennies From Heaven* and *As Time Goes By*; their favourite twelve-inch record was of songs from Ivor Novello's *The Dancing Years*; and another song that usually brought a few tears to Mum's eyes was *We'll Gather Lilacs in the Spring Again* that went on: *and walk together down an English lane, until our hearts have learnt to sing again, when you come home once more.*

At school and church of course, there was a lot of singing. Maybe it was the euphoria and optimism from the end of the war, but at that time it seemed that any gathering of people usually ended up with a good sing-song. Perhaps karaoke is the present-day successor? One of the first songs I learned at a Christmas party was the *Hokey Cokey*.

Because few people had their own car, regular organised coach outings by The Hazlemere Young Wives' Group, Sunday School and others were welcomed and everyone went, not only to the seaside, but also

30.1 The Farmbrough family coach outing.

to interesting places like Chessington or Whipsnade Zoo or Woburn
Abbey. At that time even families organised their own coach outings
and the Farmbrough family went to Clacton.

It was usually on the return journey that someone would start singing,
and before long, everyone else joined in, the words were so well known,
regular favourites were:

Roll Out the Barrel
Ten Green Bottles
It's a Long way to Tipperary
Wish Me Luck as You Wave Me Goodbye (Gracie Fields)
We'll Meet Again (Vera Lynn)
The Quotemaster's Store

31

Our Mum – Sybil's Photo Album

In the spring of 1955 Sybil Eileen (Short) Farmbrough flicks through her photograph album and looks back on various episodes in her life.

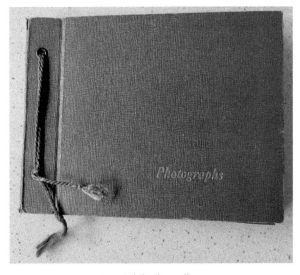

31.1 Sybil's photo album

As I think about these first few photos of my parents and grandparents, I realise they were looking out into an unknown future: they were ignorant of what was to come. It is only now, as I look back on the last thirty-odd years of my life, that I realise I am privileged to know their future, and how their lives will affect mine.

I don't remember my father; he died in 1923 when I was two years old. I was told he survived the Great War but died of tuberculosis contracted whilst in the trenches. To me he is only a photograph, wearing the uniform of the King's Rifle Regiment.

31.2 Sybil's father, Frederick Harry Short

I only remember the warmth of my mother's body and her tender touch. She died when I was four. My mother and I were living at Whitton with Granny and Grampy who were already in their mid-sixties by then. After the funeral, we went to see our relatives off on the bus and on the way back home, Granny said to Grampy:

"It's a long time since we've walked out together."

After that I continued to live with Granny and Grampy. Granny told me she applied

31.3 Sybil's mother, Lily Annie Rackstraw Short, with Sybil as a toddler

31.4 Sybil's Grampy, Edmund Rackstraw, with Bob, his Old English Sheepdog

31.5 Edmund Rackstraw and Annie Maria (Bristow) Rackstraw with Sybil

to the British Legion for a war orphan's pension and I was awarded two shillings (10p) a week, until I left school at fourteen. Granny had been a schoolteacher and governess, and now I realise how necessary it was for her to demonstrate single-mindedness and great determination throughout her life.

At Whitton I was a normal schoolgirl, I did well at school and I played with my friend, Thelma; Granny bought me a violin and paid for private lessons which I really enjoyed.

We sometimes caught the bus to visit Granny's niece, Eunice, and her family at Weybridge. I called Eunice my "Granny at Weybridge" and she had a granddaughter the same age as me, Myrtle, so we could play together.

Granny was always busy, and, when at home on sunny afternoons, she would sit at the back door and make lace, I would sit beside her and recite poetry learned at school.

There are only two pictures of me as a child; Pete was a bit luckier in that his uncle had a camera. I grew up in a typical London suburb, and my grandmother was strict but fair and I was an obedient child so I rarely strayed beyond her sphere of control. I thought this was my normal life, but it all changed in an instant.

When I was ten, I came home from school to find all the blinds in the house were drawn. Granny had died; it was such a catastrophe, I was filled with dread and I didn't know what to think nor could I imagine what would happen next.

Perhaps Grampy was suffering from shock, because for some reason it was decided Grampy couldn't look after me on his own and that I should leave Grampy at Whitton and move to Terriers near High Wycombe to live with Grampy's younger brother, William, and his wife Sarah and their family. Grampy had come from a large family, but by 1931 there were only two of his brothers still alive, Edward the elder being over eighty years and on his own.

"Why can't my Mummy come back and look after me?" I asked. No one had told me she had died six years earlier. So, then I had to cope with a double loss.

31.6 Rackstraw family tree

185

I was taken to Terriers; but found it impossible to stay without Grampy. I made so much fuss about leaving Grampy behind, that my great uncle and aunt could not ignore me.

"I won't stay here without Grampy. You only want me for the two shillings pension," I declared.

So Grampy came as well. We both squeezed into an already burgeoning household and were made to feel very uncomfortable. I shared a bed with my aunts, Ivy and Evie, but Grampy slept on a chair in the kitchen. The few bits of our household belongings from Whitton were stored in tea chests in a shed in the back garden.

I went to Priory Road School in High Wycombe and practised on my violin when I could. I covered my unhappiness by working hard at school but I was only going through the motions; I was in a strange place; all I had was Grampy.

31.7 Sybil, back row middle,
in her last year at Priory Road School, May 1935

As was usual at that time, I left school when I was fourteen and found a job in Hazlemere doing embroidery.

My whole life became meaningful when Pete arrived on the scene, and after four years of courting, Pete and I were married on 25 April 1942.

Although my full name was Sybil Eileen Short, when I was growing up, I was always called Eileen. This caused problems in the Farmbrough family because Pete's brother Jack was already married to an Eileen, so I reverted to Sybil and that was the name by which I was known for the rest of my life.

31.8 and 31.9 Pete and Sybil when they were courting

Pete and I made a home together that included Grampy, and by the end of the war we had two lovely daughters.

Just look at this picture; we are in the back garden at Finchers, it was taken on our first winter there, Diana is wearing a siren suit, even though the war was over– it was such a practical garment.

31.10 Snowman, Sybil and Diana in siren suit, 1945

How incredible that my life changed so much; and that together, Pete and I have created a comfortable home and raised two lovely daughters. We did not have a lot of money, but to us our home and family were our secret wealth, our great treasure. We were so grateful.

31.11 Diana and Mary bathing in the garden

Oh yes! This above picture reminds me, there was a heatwave. We filled two small baths with water and set them on the back lawn.

I told Diana and Mary:

"You can jump in and out and dry off in the sunshine."

They were surprised and one of them said:

31.12 Mary and Diana playing with their dolls

"The grass tickles my feet."

I had forgotten about this picture; it looks so ordinary, just two little girls playing with their dolls, but to me it means the world, the toys they play with and the freedom they have in their lives are beyond my expectations when I was their age.

31.13 Diana and Mary with snowman

I turn the page and there's this picture taken in the snow, in the front garden; Mary had just had her third birthday.

The girls made a snowman, I gave them an old hat for his head:

"Can we have some knobs of coal for his face?" they asked.

It was getting late, but how could I refuse them? Going to the shed, I took a hammer and smashed a big lump of coal. As soon as his face was complete, I said:

"The sun is going down, it's bitterly cold. We'd better get indoors."

31.14 Diana and Mary blowing bubbles

There are so many memories; it seems like yesterday we bought bubble pipes in Woolworths.

When we got home, we swirled Lux soap flakes in a small bowl.

I said:

"Fill the bowl of your pipe and blow."

Mary cried:

"I've got soap in my mouth, it tastes horrid."

I replied:

"Take a deep breath first, and then blow."

These photographs of Diana and Mary remind me how much I valued the ordinariness of their childhood. I don't consider it at all strange that I felt compelled to capture their everyday lives by taking these photographs with my box Brownie camera and make them into our family history.

Here is another picture taken in our backyard; as so often happened, after breakfast the girls followed Grampy up the garden path and were "helping" him weed the vegetable garden.

A little voice said:

31.15 Grampy with the girls

"Look at these wiggly things," and Grampy answered:

"They be worms, best hold 'em by one end. Come with me, m' little ducks, and we'll feed 'em to the 'ens."

Then they all went off up the garden path to the hen run and dropped their worms through the wire mesh and set the hens clucking and scratching. Such a simple thing, but Grampy's patience with them was built on a deep love.

When Grampy died in February 1951, I was heartbroken; he had been my constant companion, and his death was the end of a chapter in my life, the heartache and turmoil of my early years and all the subsequent ups and downs had only been made bearable by the love and devotion of two men, Grampy and Pete. But Pete and I were still young, he was thirty and I twenty-nine, and our life at Finchers continued without Grampy, and the girls gave Pete and me so much pleasure as they grew and explored the world around them.

At the same time, Pete and I want to protect the girls from the dark side of life for as long as possible and allow them to enjoy the freedom of their young lives to a greater extent than ever we did. How bittersweet to see my girls so normal and happy and taking us so much for granted; they are sure that Pete and I will always be there, that there will always be light in their lives. I want to give them that certainty but if I protect them too much, how will they cope with the inevitable dark times that lie

31.16 Diana and Mary share the swing

ahead in any life? It wasn't easy for me, but I had Grampy: will they always have each other?

As I turn the final page of my album, I realise that already Grampy has been gone for more than four years and now we are looking forward to yet another chapter in our lives: our third child is due in August. The time has come to move on and we are preparing to leave Finchers.

32

Leaving Finchers

As we were having Sunday afternoon tea in the front room one winter's day in early 1955, Mum and Dad smiled at each other, then across the table to us, and Dad said:

"We've got something to tell you."

Mum continued:

"We're going to have a new baby in the summer."

This was an unexpected piece of news; Mary and I looked at each other, our imaginations running riot. Mary spoke first:

"Will we get a boy or a girl?"

and I asked:

"What do you want Mum?"

and she replied:

"Well obviously for Dad, it would be nice to have a boy to carry on the Farmbrough name, but for me, I really don't mind whether it's a boy or a girl."

"What names will we call them?" we wondered, and more importantly,

"Where will he or she sleep?"

We had been looking for a new house before this startling piece of news. Several new housing estates were going up around High Wycombe and we favoured the three-bedroom Taylor Woodrow homes. Mum liked the fitted kitchens and modern bathrooms and Mary and I were keen on having an upstairs and each having a bedroom of our own.

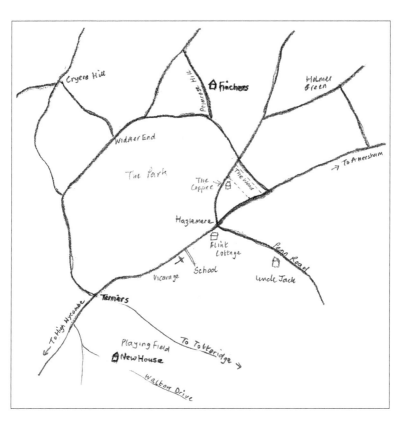

32.1 Sketch showing location of new house at Walton Drive

"This new baby will mean a change of our plans, somebody is going to have to share a bedroom," I told Mary.

Dad had paid a deposit in early January to reserve a plot of land at Terriers, backing on to a playing field, because it was convenient for the bus route into High Wycombe or on to Hazlemere – ideal for church and school; but we knew there would be a delay while the new house was built.

The arrival of the baby was confirmed at the end of January, and Mum's ankles started to swell almost immediately – she was destined to undergo a difficult pregnancy.

In February that year I passed the 11+ preliminary examination, which led on to the General Examination at the beginning of March. It was a very cold March with heavy snow; Mum had been making bridesmaids dresses for Mary and me to wear at the wedding of one of our Rackstraw cousins, Hazel. We shivered in the swirling snow for the photographs and were keen to join in the excitement of the wedding reception but couldn't stay because Mum was not feeling well. She had high blood pressure and was soon ordered to take "bed rest" at home.

Mum directed the workings of the home from her bed; she occasionally sat in the kitchen in her dressing gown and one Saturday morning towards the end of April, she said to me:

"You know how Dad likes his fruit cake to take to work."

"Yes, we all like a slice at teatime," I replied.

"I'm going to explain how to make a fruit cake, you've watched me enough times, I think you'll pick it up quite quickly," Mum was very encouraging.

"First to get ready, you must make up the Courtier and check the oven temperature, we need the oven quite hot, four hundred degrees Fahrenheit, while the cake is in." I was good at making up the fire but needed to wash my hands afterwards because of the coke dust.

"Next, you must take out the equipment and get everything ready: scales, mixing bowl and small bowl, cake tin, wooden spoon, knife and fork. Then set out the ingredients on the table: butter, sugar, eggs, flour, raisins and sultanas."

"There's so many different things," I said. "How will I remember them all?"

"When you've done it once, you will find it easier, you'll see," she continued.

"Now you must line the cake tin, grease it first with lard, and then use the margarine papers – you've seen me do this, one flat paper at the bottom and two halves round the side."

Mum was patient and encouraging, she took me through creaming the butter and sugar together and what to look for when ready, then beating in the eggs, folding in the flour and fruit, and emptying into the cake tin. She warned me to always use the oven glove and to set the alarm clock for when the cake was ready. At last, when the cake was cooked, she called Dad into the kitchen to admire the result of my hard work.

"Now Diana, I want you to make a cake every Saturday morning using the ingredients that Mr. Kneen brings, then when I'm having the baby, I'll know that you will be alright."

Shortly after this, Mum was admitted to The Shrubbery Maternity Home.

This was when we realised things were serious, and we were left on our own without Mum to tell us what to do. We both wrote to Mum in The Shrubbery:

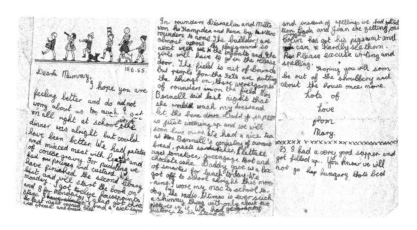

32.2 Extract from Mary's letter

Dear Mummy,

I hope you are feeling better and do not worry about us too much. I got on alright at school (most of) the dinner was alright but could have been better...

We had a nice tea at Mrs. Bennell's consisting of currant bread, paste sandwiches, lettuce and tomatoes. Greengage tart and chocolate cake. Daddy gave us a box of smarties for lunch today. The radio times is ever such a skinny ting, with only about two pictures in it...

Hoping you will soon be out of the shrubbery and about the house once more.

Lots of love from Mary

xxxxxxxxxxxxxxxxxxxxxxx

P.S. I had a very good supper and got filled up. You know we will not go hungary to bed.

By this time, I was eleven years old and Mary was ten. With the help of kind neighbours, relations and friends we managed somehow.

Extract from my letter to Mum:

Dear Mummy,

... Mrs Saunders up the road and Mrs Saunders down the road and Mrs Tilly and Mrs Bennell have all offered to do our washing, not forgetting Aunty Pauline, so we shall share the washing round and do a bit ourselves.

... Lots of love from Diana

On Saturday mornings before I made the cake, Dad got out the Hoover washing machine, an early model, it heated and turned the water, and had rubber rollers on the built-in wringer and the water dripped down into the machine. Dad, Mary and I followed the process and hung out the washing on the garden line. We called it the Chinese Laundry. Luckily our school dresses were washed and ironed elsewhere.

Mum came home again at the end of June but only for bed rest until mid-July. Our GP Dr Wilson made regular house visits and occasionally brought Mr Morris Johns the obstetrician to keep an eye on Mum. All summer long Dad continued working and Mary and I attended school. One Wednesday dinner time, we were playing in the school field, I looked up and saw Mum standing beside the headmaster, at the canteen door. I called Mary and we ran up to Mum, she handed us our comics, *Girl* and *School Friend,* and said:

"When you leave school today, you must stay on the bus and go to Aunty Pauline at Holmer Green, Dad will come and collect you when he finishes work."

"Oh Mum, what's happening?" we asked, full of dread and she gave us a hug and said:

"It'll be alright, you'll see. I'm going back to The Shrubbery, and maybe the baby will arrive early, that would be good, wouldn't it?"

"When will we see you again?" we asked, and she replied:

"Take your comics and read them at Aunty Pauline's and I'll see you again as soon as possible."

Our sister Hilary Delia was born two weeks later on 5th August in the evening while Mary and I were swimming at Maidenhead with Aunty Pauline, Uncle Reg, Geoffrey and their baby Richard (born nine months earlier). Dad took us with him on a visit to The Shrubbery Nursing Home, but we were not allowed in; we stood in the roadway, looking through a gap in the garden shrubs. A nurse brought the baby to a window for us to see, and later, Mum waved to us from a different window.

When Mum eventually came home with the baby in the middle of August, there was an idyllic late summer. Mary and I took it in turns to hold the baby, sit with her in the pram in the garden and helped dress and undress her. We had a tea party for her christening.

Mary and I were full of optimism about the new house:

"When we move, I'm going to set my ornaments out, and all my books on their own shelf." Mary had a clear idea of how it would be.

"I wonder how Nipper will like living in a street with pavements and streetlights?" I asked.

Leaving Finchers was always going to be difficult. Dad had warned us that we wouldn't be taking the hens with us, they would all be gone by Christmas. It was the only home we knew, it was the centre of our world, everything radiated from it.

32.3 Hilary's christening, October 1955
From L: Dad, Alan Barker, Reg Osborne (holding baby Richard), Fred Bowles, Geoffrey
Osborne, Pauline Osborne, Tom Barker, Connie Bowles (holding baby Hilary), Mary,
Renee, Diana, Kathleen, Rosemary Bowles, Molly Barker.

It was a bit disconcerting when Mum started turning out the loft. I found some beautiful orange and green glass Christmas tree lights in the dustbin and brought them back into the kitchen: they were old friends and bringers of magic.

"We can't keep them Diana, don't you remember we now have the lovely "Cinderella" tree lights – and they actually work?" said Mum.

Mum was up in the loft, and Mary and I were supposed to hold the stepladder and take things as they were passed down. The first thing was a three-quarter violin case. Next came a large dusty brown paper parcel tied up with ancient string. Mum had to climb down the ladder at that point because she was unable to deal with so many questions floating up through the black hole.

We brought these treasures into the kitchen and put them on the table. Our new sister, Hilary, was asleep in her carry cot next to the airing cupboard.

"Whose violin is it Mum? Where did it come from?"

We were amazed: the violin was our mother's. She opened the case; it contained a beautiful dark wooden violin, a bow with some hairs hanging, and some of the strings were broken. There were spare strings and rosin for the bow. The case was lined with green velvet and looked exquisite.

"Mum, how does it work, why don't you play it?"

Mum was fighting back the tears.

"No, I won't be able to play it now, and it's not tuned. I think I have forgotten. When I was growing up with Granny and Grampy at Whitton, Granny bought the violin for me. I had lessons from a neighbour, and I was doing really well, I got a certificate."

She started replacing the violin in its case.

"After Granny died, Grampy and I came to live at Terriers, there was no money for lessons and the violin was put away."

We knew better than to press her any further so we turned our attention to the dusty brown paper parcel.

"What's in here Mum? – Let's open it!"

She took her scissors and, most unusually, cut the string, unwrapping the parcel with tears in her voice:

"This is Granny's lace pillow; Granny was a lacemaker all her life and this is what she made her lace on."

It was a dark blue circular cushion, with bits of fabric attached; it looked intriguing, there was a short length of lace emerging behind the tarnished upright pins holding down a piece of card.

"These little stick things are called bobbins."

There was a big cluster of bobbins hanging from the pins stuck into the cushion, each dangling from the thread wound round the top; they were all slightly different shapes and colours and some had little hoops of beads hanging from the lower ends which caught the light and our attention – it was fascinating. Mum pointed to a separate padded attachment to the cushion and said:

"This is Granny's pin cushion," and then, picking up various strips of thin card, "these strips of card are the "pricking" – the lace pattern. The squiggles drawn on them are code for stitches and pinholes."

The pin cushion was attached to the pillow and the strips of card were worn with pinholes and so faded so we could hardly see any squiggle pattern at all.

"I remember Granny making lace most days, often sitting by the kitchen door in Nelson Road for the light. She would be twisting these bobbins and at the same time test me on my poems."

"That sounds so lovely, didn't you want to learn too?"

"Granny died in 1931 and that's when Grampy and I left Nelson Road; I was only about your age when it happened. It's such a long time ago; and no-one makes lace anymore, it's all machine-made these days."

I was transfixed by the thought that something our great grandmother used every day had been stored at Finchers above our heads in the loft, all our lives. Mary said:

"Fancy a pillow being so old, I wonder how things have changed over all those years?"

That was the only time Mary and I saw the lace pillow or anything to do with lacemaking.

We left Finchers on Saturday 31 December 1955.

33

Our Great Grandmother – Annie Maria Bristow and Her Lace Pillow

Lacemaking
Extract from 'Good Neighbours' by Walter Rose

The lovely craft of making lace by hand, with bobbins on a pillow, was to me, as to other outsiders… a mystery: yet to those (with the skill) it seemed to be simplicity itself, a mere adjustment of the pins on the pattern, with a curious jingling throw of the bobbins one over the other, followed by another pin adjustment, and so on. The watcher knew that the work was going forward, but the advance was almost imperceptibly slow. Undoubtedly it was love for the craft that kept them at it, not the little money earned by so many hours of devoted labour.

Annie Maria Bristow was born in 1862. Her mother, Jemima (Paine) Bristow, was a fine lacemaker from Waddesdon, a town well known for lacemaking, where Huguenot refugees had settled many years earlier and applied their skills to the cottage industry. The Bristow family lived at Cryers Hill in Buckinghamshire; her father, William Bristow, was a younger son of a family connected with farming. There were five children and Annie was the youngest, born after a thirteen-year gap. Jemima made lace pillows for all her children and she taught them to make lace; the boys made lace in the winter when there was little work on the land.

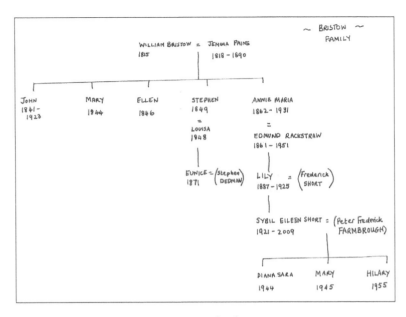

33.1 Bristow family tree

Jemima began to teach Annie:

"Before you touch your lace pillow you should first wash your hands and put on a clean pinafore. You can help me by winding the thread on these bobbins, it takes an age but it's the first step to making lace."

Annie loved watching her mother make lace and tried to follow the pairs of bobbins as they were unspooled and woven with precision to form a stitch and then the pin inserted in the appropriate place to create the pattern.

"You must learn to set out your pattern correctly and pay attention as your work goes on: it's no use getting impatient or trying to skip a section because lacemaking is not quick and you can't afford to go back to correct mistakes."

"I do like to see the lace come out behind the pins, I hope I shall be able to do as well as you," she told her mother as a small intricate work of art was created.

"I'm sure you will one day, but you need a lot of practice to keep the tension correct, so that when the pins come out the lace keeps its shape.

And you need a good light to see your work, so always sit near a lamp or window. Try to keep your feet warm, they will get cold when you sit for a long time – but not too close to the fire: any smuts could ruin your lace. When the buyer comes, he won't take it if it's not spotless."

Annie was a diligent worker and she could earn up to six pence for ten hours' work. She used some of this money to pay one penny a week for lessons from the schoolteacher at the next village, Hazlemere, because her father was adamant.

"It's a waste o' good money givin' girls an edicashun."*

"Our teacher says I'm doing well and that I'm a fast learner," Annie told her mother as they sat together with their lace pillows and bobbins clicking. Sometimes she recited common lace "tells" like:

Jack be nimble,
Jack be quick,
Jack jump over the candlestick.

As her mother went about her household chores, Annie often found herself with only her lace pillow for company, so she talked about school and anything else that came into her head, and it became her confidant and companion.

As she approached her tenth year and was completing her education, the teacher said to Annie:

"You 'ave done your lessons well, an' you 'ave a way with the lit'luns. I could do wi' your 'elp. Ask your parents if you can stay on wi' me an' teach at school."

So, Annie continued her daily walk to school but in her new role as an assistant teacher, it was a better prospect than lacemaking for a living.

Cryers Hill was a few miles outside High Wycombe and information about the outside world often came in the form of newspapers, sometimes brought back by carters or passengers from the Maidenhead train.

---

*   *(The 1870 Education Act began the process of introducing free compulsory schooling between the ages of five and thirteen, but it took many years to achieve).*

There was a well-worn towpath between Wycombe and Windsor, which followed the level valley of the River Wye to Hedsor where the Wye flows into the Thames. It was used by wagons and horses laden with stick chairs (a utilitarian chair with no padding). At Hedsor the chairs were loaded from Wycombe Wharf onto Thames barges, being shown on the bill of lading as *100 stick chairs, Windsor*; the use of this route was safe and economical. By the time the chairs reached London, they had become known as *Windsor chairs*.

One day Annie caught sight of an advertisement on the front page of the *Windsor and Eton Express* for the position of governess and companion with a family connected with Eton College and to her surprise her application was accepted. This was a big step for Annie.

She packed her few possessions, making sure her precious lace pillow and patterns were secure, and, slinging the pillow's folding cradle over her shoulder, she set off for Eton, just across the river from Windsor.

As she found her feet in her new surroundings, she continued to confide her deepest thoughts to her lace pillow whenever there was time to spare for making lace:

"You may only be a lace pillow, but you are my best friend. It's lonely being away from home for the first time and living with these strangers. When I'm making lace, I can think clearly and I always feel better."

Annie was now a proficient lacemaker. At any opportune moment, she took her pillow off its cradle and with it securely on her lap she set the bobbins dancing as she made lace to sell to a local haberdasher. Depending on the width of lace, Annie used up to twenty-four pairs of bobbins, made of yew, box, pear or bone, some with small hoops of beads, called spangles, that hung from the bottom of the bobbin. The thread was wound tightly round the top of the bobbin and it unspooled as the pattern emerged.

By 1881, Annie was nineteen years old, and her brother Stephen and his wife Louisa now lived just across the Thames at Clewer, outside Windsor, their older brother John Bristow also lived with them. Stephen and Louisa had a daughter, Eunice, who was Annie's niece but only nine years younger than Annie.

"It's so nice to have family nearby," she said to her pillow, "and Louisa is a lacemaker, so we can share patterns."

Later Annie found a position in Clewer as companion in the home of an army colonel.

"I don't have much time off work, but it is good to be even closer to Louisa and my brothers and I can spend more time with young Eunice," she told her pillow.

A few years later she shared with the pillow her excitement about meeting a young chap who worked with the horses at Home Farm on the Windsor Estate:

"That Edmund Rackstraw, he's quiet, sensitive and considerate, not like a lot of those rowdy types in the town; and he comes from Hazlemere where I went to school."

Soon they were walking out, sometimes down the Long Walk at Windsor as far as The Copper Horse, and sometimes along the river to Boveney Lock. Before long, Edmund (then twenty-five) and Annie (twenty-four) were married and a daughter, Lily Annie, was born the next year at Windsor in 1887. Annie's employer gave her and Edmund a wedding present of etched Georgian wine glasses, which Annie treasured for the rest of her life.

When Lily was asleep and she could make an inch of lace, she cried into her pillow:

"Naturally, I've lost my position because I'm married, and finding somewhere to live, and a job for Edmund isn't easy."

The little family moved back to their roots at Hazlemere and Edmund worked in the furniture industry for a while; but factory work didn't suit Edmund, so, leaving Annie and Lily at Hazlemere, he tried elsewhere and by 1897 when Lily was ten, Annie greeted her pillow with some better news:

"Edmund's sent for me and Lily to join him, now he's got a job with horses in Chiswick. It's only one room in a shared house but at least we can be together. What a difficult time it's been, they say it's been hard for everyone."*

Once the family were living together at Short Road, Chiswick,

---

* *(This period was later called The Great Depression of British Agriculture).*

Annie confided her ambition to her pillow: "I do hope Lily will find more opportunities at school here in Chiswick and make new friends, she deserves a bright future." Annie was optimistic, and indeed, Lily soon adjusted her country ways to fit in with her newfound friends.

A few years later when Edmund was approaching forty, he found work as a council carter and with accommodation at Pelican Cottages, Ham Moor on the banks of the River Wey near Weybridge. It was an ideal location, close to Edmund's work, and with direct access to the river.

"I think we shall be happy here," Annie told everyone she knew, and Edmund agreed:

"Now we have some land, we shall be able to grow our own vegetables; we could keep a few hens."

The lower part of the River Wey from Godalming to Weybridge (where it joins the River Thames) is called The Wey Navigation, and with the constant movement of horse-drawn barges up and down the Navigation, life at Ham Moor was far from dull and, at last, more settled than at any time since Edmund and Annie's marriage. They could walk into Addlestone or Weybridge and for a short walk on a summer evening, stroll to the first lock, just up the river at Lock Mill.

"We don't have many outings, but we do enjoy being seen walking out together," Annie thought to herself, as she and Edmund strolled contentedly beside the water.

Annie's niece Eunice was now married to Stephen Dedman and they had three children just a few years younger than Lily, all living close by in Weybridge.

"It's always a treat to go into Weybridge and see Eunice and the children," she said to her old friend, her lace pillow.

Annie always encouraged Lily to learn the intricacies of lacemaking:

"Just as my mother taught me, you should always have clean hands and a clean pinafore before you think about touching the pillow," she instructed Lily.

"You know I want to be like you and make beautiful lace," said Lily. "I'm already good at helping with winding your bobbins and sewing up the loose ends on the finished lace."

By 1901, when Lily was fourteen years old, she was apprenticed to a dressmaker, working long hours on low pay.

"Now Lily's away most of the time, I can help Edmund learn to read and write," Annie schemed as she twisted her bobbins. "I've sent away for a book about first aid for horses, I know he will take to that."

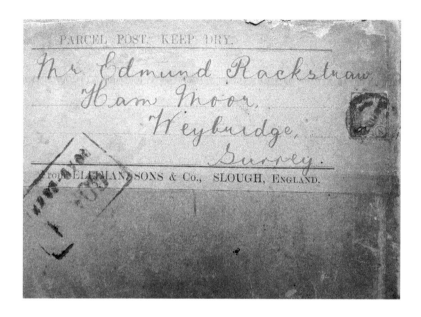

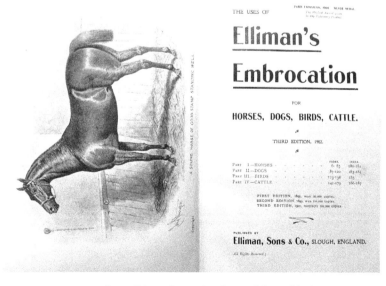

33.2 and 33.3 Edmund's parcel and animal first aid book

33.4 Lily Rackstraw, 1910 (aged 23)

Edmund (born in 1861) was the sixth of eight children and had grown up at Hazlemere in Buckinghamshire. The story is that when he was fourteen years old (in 1875), he left home and joined the militia. Too young to fight, he became a medical orderly and was soon despatched to South Africa as part of a force to secure British interests. There, his experiences caused a total aversion to conflict, and possibly what today might be labelled post-traumatic stress disorder. Wretched and demoralised, he had made his way back home by 1881; and thereafter became a life-long pacifist with a disgust for the army, soldiers and war.

From the turn of the century, his life with Annie at Ham Moor had been settled and he kept his feelings under control, until the Great War broke out and his family faced a new threat. Their daughter, Lily, had been courted by Frederick Harry Short, a young market gardener from Hersham. He enlisted with The Kings Royal Rifle Corps and, in 1915, before leaving for the War on the Western Front, Fred and Lily were married. Edmund was filled with dread and loathing, and this set father and daughter at odds:

"No good'll come from the army or any soldier," said Edmund, pacing up and down.

"There's a thin line between soldiering and evil; you'll find out violence begets violence." Edmund was wringing his hands, and continued:

"O dear O Lor', it makes my blood run cold to think of our Lily having anything to do with a soldier."

Edmund's outspoken opinions against the war not only caused a rift with Lily but were unpopular with his workmates as well as with the neighbours at Ham Moor. Annie suffered untold anguish:

"It breaks my heart to see them both so stubborn and hurtful," she cried into her lace pillow, as with great dexterity she wove the threads from her bobbins into a good length of lace.

"I am torn in two by this disagreement, and it's clear Edmund is beside himself," but later she sobbed: "It's worse than I could ever imagine, Edmund has lost his job and our cottage that comes with it."

"What have I done to deserve this?" cried Annie. "Do all these years here at Ham Moor count as nothing?"

Annie and Lily went to stay with Eunice in Weybridge, and Edmund found work at a brewery in Fulham, and possibly solace, with the dray horses, while living next to the stables.

At Weybridge, Eunice, Annie and Lily shared their highs and lows as the Great War dragged on. A great many tears were shed over the next few years.

"How grateful I am to have such a good friend in Eunice," she confided to her pillow, "but she too has her worries with her son, Fred, on the Western Front, and there's no news."

Miraculously by 1918 both Fred Dedman and Fred Short came home from the war.

Toward the end of the Great War, Edmund found another job as a carter, at Twickenham, and he and Annie eventually resettled at 76 Nelson Road, Whitton. After the war, Fred and Lily came to live as part of the household, but all was not well, Fred had been diagnosed with tuberculosis and ill health made it difficult for him to work.[*]

Nevertheless, two years later, in August 1921, Lily gave birth to their daughter, Sybil.

---

[*] *The British Legion claim that 55,000 servicemen returned with TB, and little effective treatment was available.*

33.5 Lily Rackstraw Short

"It's such a relief to have us all together under one roof," Annie told her lace pillow. "Fred does a bit of market gardening when he can, and even Fred and Edmund rub along together now, because of the baby."

Before Sybil was two years old, her father Fred succumbed to his TB, and then, only two years later, it became apparent that Lily had cancer of the stomach. By 1925 she too was dead.

Annie, then aged sixty-three, sat making lace, and, as a delicate edging of lace emerged, she confided in her pillow:

"After all the suffering of the War, it's hard to accept the loss of Lily, my only daughter, this feels deeper and more raw. I am diminished by it." Later she added: "And now I must take on the task of raising Sybil, my poor little granddaughter, she's only four years old. I am sixty-three, and the world is changing, what can I possibly give her to guide her through life?"

And so, she sat and twisted her bobbins and created a few more inches of lace. Then she rose and with a look of resignation said:

"I must do what I've always done. I must teach Sybil to value the truth, conduct her affairs with prudence and good manners, be determined and hold fast to her ideals and above all, meet adversity with stoicism."

As Sybil grew, she enjoyed visits with Annie, her grandmother, to the Dedman family still living at Weybridge; Sybil called Eunice her "Granny at Weybridge". Sometimes Sybil went to stay for a few days in the summer, when Eunice, wanting to make Sybil feel part of the family, kept a bag of toiletries aside (flannel, hair comb and toothbrush), especially for Sybil's use.

Eunice's son, Fred Dedman, had survived being gassed in the Great War and returned to his trade as a shoemaker in Weybridge. Sybil liked to sit with her Uncle Fred in his shoemaker's shop; he remembered her parents and could talk to her about them. One of his customers was Roger Bannister, the first man to run a mile in under four minutes. Uncle Fred and his wife Kate lived in the centre of Weybridge with their two children, Myrtle and Donald, who were much the same age as Sybil. Myrtle and Sybil were good friends.

There were other occasions, where, for an afternoon outing, Annie took Sybil by bus to visit Kew Gardens. On summer evenings they walked down Nelson Road to hear the Royal Army School of Music perform at Kneller Hall.

As the orphaned daughter of a veteran of the Great War, Sybil was entitled to an allowance of two shillings a week during her childhood. With this Annie bought a violin for Sybil and arranged music lessons; she made sure Sybil had plenty to occupy her time. While Annie was making lace, she encouraged Sybil to learn poetry by rote; they recited together poems such as 'The Pied Piper of Hamlin' or 'Cargoes'.

At home in Whitton, Annie would sit with her lace pillow on her lap by the kitchen door, and whisper:

"As I sit here with Sybil at my side, it's so easy to recall my time with Lily all those years ago; it's uncanny how they examine the delicacy of the work and appear to share the joy I feel as I move the bobbins and pins and the beauty of the lace is revealed."

When it came to lacemaking, Sybil's fascination was deep enough to detect an empathy between Annie and her lacemaker's pillow. Sitting with her as the bobbins danced, and the threads unspooled, just as they always had done throughout Annie's life, she could discern her grandmother's pleasure as another small work of art was created.

To Sybil, Annie was "Granny". She died suddenly of a heart attack in 1931 when Sybil was nearly ten years old. Life at Nelson Road ended abruptly and amid the chaos the lace pillow was wrapped in a brown paper parcel, along with the bobbins, pins and patterns and securely tied up with string. Sybil was taken first, and Edmund followed; they left Whitton with a few possessions packed in a tea chest and went to live in Buckinghamshire.

Lacemaking
Extract from 'Good Neighbours' by Walter Rose

For those who made lace it seemed to be reward enough when lovers of the beautiful, bent over a pillow and examined the delicacy of the work, for then they knew the joy that is always felt when two kindred loves fuse in a common object.

Acknowledgements

I am grateful for the opportunity presented by lockdown at the start of the pandemic in March 2020: during that first April, my tutor and mentor, Sue Burge, guided me (and my husband Mike) through daily email prompts and opened our minds to creative journal writing, and importantly, distracted us from the relentless and distressing news of the pandemic. By May 2020, I had conceived a plan to expand a few scribbled notes into a memoir of my early life. I joined Sue's 'Writing Cloud', a tutored creative writing group, and somehow, over the next two years, I produced a two-thousand-word story once a month. As these stories emerged, as well as diverting my husband and me, they provided entertainment for my sisters on our weekly zoom meetings.

Along the way I received help, encouragement, and support from many people, organisations, and groups, including the following:

D H Gantzel, author of "Hazlemere", for use of the image 06.01 of Flint Cottage.

Allan Power, High Wycombe Library, for providing press cuttings from the *Bucks Free Press* about the murder in Chapter 16.

Dr Catherine Grigg, Wycombe Museum, for suggesting useful contacts and for fondly recalling my father as a volunteer at the museum.

Sally Mason, Buckinghamshire Archives, for information about the murder in Chapter 16.

Anthony Mealing Dip Arch RIBA, AABC, for permission to use his research on how Windsor chairs got their name.

Mike Dewey of 'Sharing Wycombe Old Pictures' (SWOP) – www. swop.org.uk, a fertile source of photographs of old Wycombe and the surrounding district – for permission to use images 12.01, 20.01 20.02, from the *Bucks Free Press* and image 31.07 from High Wycombe Society.

Members of SWOP Facebook Group who quickly named the shoe shop on Frogmoor, in Chapter 20.

Bill Brakes of Lavender Lace Makers for generously providing advice on lacemaking.

Priscilla Cassam for her kind encouragement in the use of *The Months* by Sara Coleridge.

Peter Craik and Nicholas Wall of the Vaughan Williams Memorial Library.

Cambridge University Press for licence to use epigrams in Chapter 33.

Cousin David Farmbrough of Wisconsin for generously sharing his research into Joseph Monk Farmbrough in Chapter 26, and permission to use images 24.06, 26.03, 26.04, and 26.05 by Will Farmbrough (now © 2022 David Farmbrough) and used with his enthusiastic permission.

Cousin Molly Francis, always encouraging and helpful for correcting spellings and filling in gaps used in Chapter 24.

Cousin Renee Jalabert, for her encouraging help and for providing background information used in Chapter 24.

Sister Mary Mayes, who drew the map image 02.01. After reading each story when first written she invariably said: "I don't remember any of this!" and then promptly helped fill out the story.

Sister Hilary Farmbrough, who read each story when first written and carefully edited the first complete draft.

Father Peter Farmbrough (1920-1998), who at the suggestion of Hilary's husband, David O'Neale, recorded on cassette tape memories of his early life in Hazlemere.

Mother Sybil Farmbrough (1921-2009), who very occasionally let slip a snippet of information about her early life.

Without the help and encouragement of my husband Mike Brindle, this adventure would have failed miserably at several critical stages. We have found that his patience and critical questioning during the reading and re-reading of every story has brought us closer as we shared the re-living of those times so long ago. I am glad to have taken this opportunity to pass on my recollections.

Most images used were taken by family members and found when clearing our parents' home. Every effort has been made to trace copyright holders and to obtain their permission for the use of copyright material. The author apologises for any errors or omissions in the above list and would be grateful if notified of any corrections that should be incorporated in any future reprints or editions of this book.

Bibliography

These are the books I have kept by me and referenced.

Beechey, Winifred, *The Rich Mrs. Robinson,* Oxford University Press (1984)

Gantzel, DH, *Hazlemere,* Barnham Press Limited (1987)

Rose, Walter, *Good Neighbours*, Cambridge University Press (1942)

About the Author

Diana Farmbrough grew up near High Wycombe in Buckinghamshire. She left school at sixteen and worked as a secretary. After moving to Norfolk at the age of thirty, she undertook training as a Legal Executive and spent the rest of her working life in Local Government.

When We Lived at Primrose Hill is Diana's first book, written as a collection of short stories during the Covid pandemic to amuse her sisters at their zoom meetings.

She lives in King's Lynn and is happily married. She shares an interest in photography and a busy family life with her husband.

Ingram Content Group UK Ltd.
Milton Keynes UK
UKHW022049040423
419639UK00006B/160/J